P9-CAY-122

GIVE TO LIVE

HOW GIVING CAN CHANGE YOUR LIFE

Douglas M. Lawson, Ph.D.

ALTI
PUBLISHING

Library of Congress Catalog Card number 91-072216

ISBN 0-9625399-3-7 Hardcover
     0-9625399-9-6 Softcover

Printed in the United States of America

10 9 8 7 6 5 4 3 2 1

For information or additional copies
contact: ALTI Publishing
           4180 La Jolla Village Drive
           Suite 520
           La Jolla, California 92037
           Tel: (619) 452-7703
           FAX: (619) 452-6841
           Book Orders: 1(800) 284-8537
Printed on recycled paper.

If you want happiness
  for an hour—take a nap.
If you want happiness
  for a day—go fishing
If you want happiness
  for a month—get married
If you want happiness
  for a year—inherit a fortune.
If you want happiness
  for a lifetime—help someone else.

CHINESE PROVERB

CONTENTS

ACKNOWLEDGMENTS

Writing a book like *Give to Live* was the direct result of a gift to me—of the writing and editing talents of many dedicated people. I want to single out for a special word of gratitude the assistance of Dan Fitzgibbon and Adam McCoy. Without Dan's ability to translate my spoken words into readable prose, and Adam's talent at organizing and rewriting, this book would not have been possible.

I also want to thank Cynthia Glacken for introducing me to Dan and to Renni Browne. Renni, Adam, and others with her remarkable company, The Editorial Department—notably Jane Rafal and Dave King—brought a great deal of professionalism and hard work to the project.

Give to Live has been a part of my presentations at seminars and lectures for years. My debt of gratitude to the many participants who shared their observations on giving is beyond calculation. As for my professional colleagues, friends, and clients through the years who have helped me, I truly wish I had the space to list their names. But to several I owe a special word of thanks: Art Frantzreb, Dr. Robert Schuller, Dr. John Haggai, Ronda Johnson, David Grubbs, and Ann Grimm, who gave me the book's title.

For the gift of the many weekends and evenings to write and edit, I want to thank my wife, Barbara Taylor. She also deserves the credit for introducing me to Manuel Arango, founder and president of the Mexican Center for the Study of Philanthropy. It was he who took the mighty risk in arranging for ALTI Publishing to bring out this unknown author's work. To him and his faith in me I owe a great deal.

Beyond these special people who encouraged me in the writing of this book, I would like to acknowledge the example of true giving my mother and father set for me as a child. This book really started with the spirit they shared with me.

And finally, I want the world to know that without the unconditional gift of love to me every day on the part of a white eight-pound maltese dog named Popcorn, I might never have persevered.

FOREWORD
Dr. Robert H. Schuller

Doug Lawson has been a colleague and friend of mine for over fifteen years. I met him in 1976 on Maundy Thursday, as we set out to begin raising the $20 million needed to build the Crystal Cathedral.

Our first professional visit together was to John Crean, founder and chairman of Fleetwood Enterprises, a Fortune 500 company based in Riverside, California. Mr. Crean called me the next day, Good Friday, to say he would be happy to be the first $1 million giver to the Crystal Cathedral.

Doug Lawson is largely responsible for our having raised the balance of the money for this magnificent building. He is still a consultant to our ministry, his wise counsel valued by us all. Early in our relationship he taught me his philosophy of the joy of giving, and it has been etched on my mind and ministry ever since.

An ordained United Methodist minister, Dr. Lawson began his ministry at the age of eighteen by building a Methodist church in Hampton, Virginia. He went on to earn a Ph.D. from Duke University in religion and history, but it was at that little church in Hampton that Doug began to develop his philosophy of giving. That philosophy has been the key to a remarkable career in which he has raised literally hundreds of millions of dollars for worthy causes and charities in America and all over the world.

Dr. Lawson is one of the most important figures in the extraordinary American world of generous giving. And in these pages he shares with the reader his years of experience. We have plenty of books on fund raising, but very few on giving and none that tell us how giving benefits the giver. *Give to Live* is a pioneering book that is badly needed by all of us as individuals and as a society.

In *Give to Live*, Doug shows how scientists are coming around to one of the most important lessons I have learned in all my years in the ministry. People come to life—become fully alive, aware, and joyful—when they help others. It is one of the great teachings of the Christian, Jewish, and Moslem religions that God loves us when we love each other, when we share His love with other human beings.

Jesus says, "It is better to give than to receive." And St. Paul says, "God loves a cheerful giver." And new researchers agree: giving is the key to abundant life. When we share with others, we are sharing the love of God with them. And the great secret of God's love is that the more we share it, the more of it there is to share.

Give to Live tells the inspiring and exciting story of what happens to us when we give. We deepen and enrich our own lives to an extraordinary degree as we give to others. Giving helps us share in God's work of creation. When we link ourselves to each other through volunteer work and charitable giving we are linking ourselves to the love of God.

The effect of giving, sharing, volunteering, and working for a better world is both wonderfully simple and wonderfully practical. We have better lives. And as Doug Lawson makes so clear, our lives are made better in every possible way—physically, psychologically, and emotionally as well as morally.

This is a great story. I hope you read Doug's book with care and put its wisdom into practice. Your life will be better, and so will the world.

INTRODUCTION

Many of us give up our lives by the time we reach twenty-one. We don't go to an early grave, thanks to medical science, but far too many of us lose our life force, our direction, our purpose. The challenge is age-old: how are we to live and enjoy our lives fully? The threefold approach set forth in this book is one practical solution to that dilemma.

First, we need a *purpose* fit to live for. Second, we need to become comfortable with and accept who we are—we need to be *selves* fit to live with. Finally, we need a *faith* fit to live by.

So how do we find this meaning? How do we develop a self that we can be comfortable with? Most important, just where do we find faith that can empower and enrich us and others? Our library shelves are filled with popular psychology books, quick-fix menus, and obscure rituals that promise heaven on earth, a magic land of plenty, a quiet place where we can hear our heart sing. Of those few books that make good on these promises, most are simply ancient material dressed up in contemporary clothes. Their theories rarely break new ground and even more rarely offer measurable evidence to back up the theories.

Give to Live does not promise more than it can deliver. Nor does it present itself as the only solution to the troubles that beset us. What it does do is offer you a new way of looking at your life. This angle of approach arises out of startling new information about the measurable, proven benefits you can gain from giving. These benefits include longer life, a lower level of stress, a stronger immune system, a stronger heart—literally as well as fig-uratively. The book outlines a program, a series of steps anyone can take that can lead you to greater emotional well-being, enhanced ability to cope with daily problems, and heightened appreciation of your own life.

Give to Live is based on the experiences of thousands of people who have chosen to give of themselves in a consis-tent and committed way. It tells you what you can do for others and what benefits you can derive from helping them. It is my intent to share with you what I have learned from many, many people who have found effec-tive ways to increase dramatically their physical well-being, their emotional happiness, and their spiritual har-mony.

In this book you will learn what some of the most honored medical doctors, psychotherapists, and scientists of our age have to say about the benefits of extending yourself to benefit others. Now we have new evidence that shows how we can help heal ourselves when we reach out to help others.

Give to Live looks at the entire philanthropic process: the extent of giving (we are a phenomenally, uniquely generous nation), what motivates us to give, and what sabotages our efforts and deprives us of much of the richness of the experience. It lays out effective steps you can take to get involved, increase your ability to make a real difference in the world, and enjoy the philanthropic journey.

Give to Live holds forth a bold promise: if you want more out of your life and are willing to take some simple steps, you can have a richer, fuller, happier existence. I invite you to try the program of action set forth in these pages. I invite you to believe me when I say that you have everything to gain and absolutely nothing to lose from a life of giving.

O·N·E

A TROUBLED
BUT GIVING NATION

A Search for Meaning

Deeds of giving are the very foundation of the world.
The Torah

All is not well in Camelot. Millions of Americans are
profoundly unhappy with their lives. Many are isolated,
unconnected, adrift, lost. Family ties are tenuous. Divorce, disease, and debt race like plagues through city and
suburb. Tension, aggression, and the scramble to survive
take a terrible toll. Marital and family problems, health
problems, work problems, failures, financial setbacks,
loneliness, and despair seem to form an endless river
threatening to submerge us. Hostility, crime, and alienation seem to outpace progress.

Our problems are legion, and many of us feel increasingly helpless as our control slips and stress mounts. Economic hardship and declining income make guests of
anxiety and apprehension in many homes that once
seemed secure. Untold numbers of Americans suffer and
yet persevere. If you listen carefully, you can hear the
urgency in their voices when they describe what they
want: freedom from illness, financial security, safety, happiness, contentment, peace of mind. . . . Above all they
want some sense of control over our increasingly bewildering world. They want a secure, meaningful existence.

What we are experiencing is not new. In his first ser-
mon, many centuries ago, the Buddha described much of

what is now confronting us. To a small group of followers he set forth his Noble Truths. The first: that man's existence is full of conflict, dissatisfaction, sorrow, and suffering. The second: that suffering begins in our own selfish desires, craving for pleasure and avoidance of pain. In short, we are the architects of our own difficulties.

Some two hundred years ago, the French educator Alexis de Tocqueville came to America to study our newly independent republic. In *Democracy in America* he pointed to elements of colonial life that still describe Americans today: "I have seen the freest and best educated of men in circumstances the happiest to be found in the world. Yet it seemed to me that a cloud habitually hung on their brow and they seemed serious and almost sad in their pleasures. They never stop thinking of the good things they have not got. They clutch everything and hold nothing fast."

We have grown more knowledgeable and secure over the last two hundred years, but I suspect that our sadness has deepened, envy has increased, and the furrowed brow has given way to a perpetual scowl. Our "pursuit of happiness" seems to lead us into more and more unsettling times.

What seems to pull us back from the brink of despair and disillusionment is our energy, our belief in good, our faith, and our dogged determination. The forces that hammer at us have turned us into a nation of seekers. Part of our search has been prompted by a sense that much of our lives is empty, confusing, monotonous, unrewarding. We search for meaning and inspiration, for a workable formula that can lead us to a joyful, contented, satisfying existence.

As a nation we seem almost to have forgotten how to enjoy life, unable to take a minute and receive the smell of spring flowers or the sight of a glowing sunset. When we lose joy we lose some of our freedom, some of our sense of community. And because we sense this loss, we try mightily to recapture it.

In our dissatisfaction many of us turn to religion, to enlightened teachers, gifted therapists, or charismatic leaders. In increasing numbers, we find strength and guidance in support groups and we read self-help books and tapes. For most of us, the religious community has become the place where we search for meaning and clarity—two thirds of American adults now attend religious services. The influence of this religious guidance may make it the most positive force operating in America today. It nurtures and directs us, tempers discontent, quiets the hostile heart. The religious community at its best promotes solidarity, brotherly love, compassion, and acceptance. It supports us in moments of distress and asks us to do the same for our neighbor.

Through the ages, people have tried to eliminate conflict and suffering, to experience lives of value and purpose. Many solutions have been advanced over many centuries. One that has endured calls on us to "do unto others as we would have them do unto us." This "golden" rule is the primary law of peaceful coexistence. Partly out of compassion and responsibility, partly for survival or self-protection, people support the institutions they cherish.

Churches, synagogues, meeting houses, and mosques act as counterbalances to the acquisitive, self-centered, aggressive spirit that undermines our higher purpose. The cult of rugged individualism—man alone against the world—is challenged by many institutions but especially by the religious community. The truth is, we cannot survive and find enjoyment through isolation and personal power. A successful life, full of meaning, calls for close cooperation, respect for the rights of others, and compassion. The Golden Rule is still the best path to a rewarding life. As Dr. William Redford puts it in his book, *The*

Trusting Heart, "The core of Christianity and all the other major religions is that we should treat others as we would like them to treat us."

Since you are reading this book, you are likely to be looking for meaning, a better reason for living—and way of living—your life. In your search, give some thought to these questions:

- How satisfied are you with the way your life is unfolding?
- What problems and issues trouble you the most?
- Are you really happy with your present state of health?
- Is there room for more giving in your life, and if so, what's holding you back?
- Would you like to receive more attention, affection, and love in your life?
- Do you believe that giving and sharing who you are (and what you have) could make you measurably happier and healthier?
- How much of your life is "on hold" waiting for something to happen?

Think about your answers and where you are in your life. Then read on. You will find solutions in the following pages.

A Caring Spirit

Love is not getting but giving.

Marie Dressler

Despite all our tension, discontent, and the thundering forces of acquisitiveness, America is the most giving and caring nation on the face of the globe. Our generosity and benevolence far surpass that of all other nations—apparently our well-publicized troubles have not blunted our compassion and concern for others. During my thirty-seven years of work with nonprofit organizations, twenty-five of them as a professional fund raiser, I have watched annual philanthropic giving grow from $15 billion to almost $115 billion.

Through lean and prosperous years alike, Americans have always given more to charity than they did the previous year. Boom or bust, we as a nation care more than ever about the welfare—the health, education, recreation, and spiritual needs—of others. Two hundred years ago, De Tocqueville singled out our forefathers' commitment to help, house, and nurture neighbors. He wrote with amazement about our sense of community and charitable actions, about the way they strengthened us as a new society. And the words de Tocqueville wrote then are still true today.

Since the birth of our republic, philanthropy has brought us together and given many of us a sense of purpose. Americans have consistently shown compassion for others along with a passion for freedom.

I believe benevolence to be a powerful force that has contributed to our success as a nation, our concern for others (despite our own problems) to be an expression of our highest ideals. I'm also convinced that the giving spirit has done much to bring together the diverse populations of our vast country. Our giving ways have become a palpable demonstration of our willingness to help our neighbor.

Caring and sharing in America take many forms, from volunteer efforts to feed the homeless to the benevolence of families like the Annenbergs, who recently donated $50 million to the United Negro College Fund. Our donations help preserve the wilderness and make it possible for parents to stay with their children during cancer treatment. The list of benevolent acts is almost endless. Where there is a need, there is almost always a concerned community group of or institution ready to help.

When we see a need we often give our time, talent, and emotional energy along with money. The sheer scale of our giving is staggering. In 1989, according to *Giving USA*, more than $115 billion was given to charity in America. Corporations and foundations accounted only for approximately one tenth of all giving—and the greatest amount by far of that incredible sum was given by individuals:

Source	Percent of Total $ Donated
Individuals	84
Bequests	6
Foundations	6
Corporations	4

But statistics do not capture the spirit, personal involvement, or concern that attend these gifts.

When Hurricane Hugo devastated the low-lying areas of the southeastern United States in 1989—flooding communities, destroying homes, and leaving thousands homeless—the entire nation responded. Individuals and corporations gave money, talent, and labor to help Hugo's victims. If you travel through that area today, you will find new homes standing where old ones were destroyed. Many of these were built with money donated to nonprofit organizations like Habitat for Humanity, one of whose volunteer workers is former President Jimmy Carter.

Some people contribute "gifts in kind," such as art, real estate, food, and clothing. Gracious old mansions in their declining years become orphanages or residences for the homeless. Private art collections are donated to museums for all to enjoy. Rock music stars donate their time and talents to raise money for financially failing farmers, AIDS victims, and the homeless. A movie star, Celeste Holm, charges 50¢ for her autograph and gives the money to a famine relief organization. Paul Newman gives the profits from the food products bearing his name to charity. Garrison Keillor gives the profits from his best-selling book to public radio. These are just a few of the ways people from all walks of life express their concern and compassion.

A wonderful image of sharing from the American past is a traditional "barn raising." In early rural America a barn was essential, and a farmer whose barn burned down was in deep trouble. But if a storm, fire, or flood destroyed the barn, the whole community immediately banded together to raise a new one. It mattered little that the stricken farmer was of a different faith, or from a different homeland, or even a virtual stranger. He was in trouble, his neighbors cared, and their care and concern bonded them together.

Barn raisings may have disappeared from the rural scene, but the spirit lives on. While economic conditions and lifestyles are very different today, the compassion and caring that nourished early America are still evident in the fabric of everyday American life. Institutions have changed and problems are more complex, but the response is largely the same. The affluent help the impoverished, those who can read teach the illiterate, corporations support communities, the elderly are protected by the young, and those who serve a loving God out of faith nurture the spirit of their religion. There is a richness in the fabric of American life—rooted in giving—that is present in good times and in bad.

In Houston, Texas, during the sharp decline in oil prices in the mid-1980s, individuals and corporations alike were going bankrupt faster than new jobs could be created. The numbers of the homeless swelled as whole families joined the ranks of the desperate and destitute. The corporate leaders and foundations of Houston, along with concerned citizens like George Bush, reached into their almost empty pockets to build one of the finest homeless shelters for women and children in America. It was my privilege to be a part of that fund-raising campaign, and if you visit the Star of Hope Family Shelter, you will see not just a well-constructed haven but a tribute to America's giving spirit.

The table below from *Giving USA* shows who were the beneficiaries of the $115 billion donated in 1989.

Who Benefits from Giving	Percent of 1989 Total $ Given
Religion	47.4
Human Services	9.9
Education	9.3
Health	8.7
Arts/Culture/Humanities	6.5
Public/Society Benefit	3.2
All other organizations	15.0

Americans give most of their money to religious organizations. In 1989 such gifts increased about 13% over the previous year, while contributions to health and education reported only modest gains.

The Independent Sector reported some positive facts about American giving in a 1988 study entitled "Giving and Volunteering in the United States":

- Fully three-quarters of U.S. households contributed to charitable organizations.
- The average household contribution was $734 annually, about 2% of total family income. Ninety-five million households gave money to charities
- Total individual contributions were 31% greater than donations two years earlier.
- An astonishing one in every seven households contributed 5% or more of their income to charity.
- Giving is as concentrated as wealth. Just as a large proportion of the nation's wealth is concentrated in the hands of a fortunate few, only 20% of all U.S. households accounted for 70% of all contributions.
- The poor are more compassionate than the wealthy. Moderate- and low-income Americans contributed *proportionately* more of their income to charity. Families earning less than $10,000 annually gave 2.8% of their income to charity while those with incomes of $100,000 or more contributed 2.1%.
- Age strongly influences contributions. Contributors in the twenty-five to thirty-four age bracket gave 2.1% of their annual income while those sixty-five to seventy-four gave twice as much (4.2%).

It's inspiring to wade through the Independent Sector statistics and uncover such reassuring findings as these:

- Of those people seventy-five and older, 22% reported that they only "had enough income to cover their basic necessities"—yet they gave 2.2% of their meager income ($267 on average) to charity.
- Among all elderly donors, another one third claimed to have "only a small amount left over to spend on other things," yet despite their near poverty they

contributed 3.1% of their annual income (about $429).

- Oddly enough, about one fourth of U.S. contributors have no clear idea how their giving compares to that of others like themselves. But their typical annual contribution is just under $1,000, above average for all contributors.

- One of the most important factors influencing how much a person gives is attendance at religious services. Those who regularly attend services accounted for a whopping 70 percent of all giving (2.4% of their income). Those who don't attend services gave only 0.8% of their income annually.

A religious or spiritual connection is clearly the driving force behind much of America's benevolence. It is also a major impetus to volunteering. People who attend religious services weekly are the most likely to volunteer. According to Virginia Hodgkinson of *Independent Sector*, "The schools stopped teaching moral values a long time ago. Mom's working, so there's not as much guidance from home. Parents are turning to religion for help." *Newsweek* reported in December of 1990 that children are leading their parents back to churches and synagogues. And as Virginia Hodgkinson and Robert Wuthnow point out in *Faith and Philanthropy in America*, the linkage between religion and giving in America remains solid.

The good news is that charitable contributions in America continue to outpace inflation and economic downturns. The bad news is that our need for services grows greater with each passing day.

America is a giving nation at its heart. It is this caring spirit that forms the foundation upon which the best of this nation is built.

Philanthropy Is People-to-People

> Our work brings people face to face with love. To us
> what matters is an individual. To get to love the person
> we must come in close contact with him.
>
> *Mother Teresa*

Some people express their compassion by donating in response to an "arm's length" solicitation, an appeal letter, or a telethon with an 800 number. But for most people the essence of giving is one-on-one contact. Personal involvement is most rewarding, whether it is providing food for the homeless, organizing a recreation program for blind children, or pitching in to clean up a community after a flood. No matter how intensely the media depicts the needs or the benefits of monetary contributions, personal contact adds an extra dimension.

Hands-on involvement, volunteer effort, personal devotion are what provide the most benefit to both recipient and volunteer. The miracle of people-to-people involvement lies in seeing your mission succeed—reaching the people you help, making a real difference by your own presence and effort. Consider some findings from the 1988 Independent Sector study of how we are already involved:

- About 54% of all adult Americans claimed they undertook some kind of volunteer work, donating an average of 4.7 hours per week.
- Most of this volunteer effort was formal (scheduled work within an organization). The combined efforts of these 98 million adults produced a staggering annual total of almost 20 billion volunteer hours—which is the equivalent of the efforts of 9 million full-time employees. The dollar value of this effort is about

$150 billion yearly—a sum that surpasses the total annual amount of monetary giving. Americans are clearly interested in helping people by getting personally involved as well as by giving money.

· Leaving aside fund-raising efforts, the most active areas of personal involvement consisted of donating time and energy:

Personally Gave Time To	Percent of Volunteers
Religious organizations	45
Educational institutions	29
Youth Development	16
Human Services	14
Health organizations	24
Recreation, sports activities	22

Not surprisingly, the typical volunteer reported giving time to at least two organizations in the past year.

· There is a strong linkage between volunteering and giving. Those who both gave and volunteered contributed an average of $1,021 to charity. Those who did not volunteer contributed an average of $357.

· Only about one-third of people who were not members of a religious organization volunteered. But more than 60% of members of religious organizations volunteered.

· People offer many reasons for volunteering. Some are carrying on traditions that have long guided their families. Others participate because they are asked by relatives, friends, members of their community, or people who represent a cause with which they identify. Still others become involved because they believe their efforts will benefit friends or relatives.

- While millions of people give billions of hours in volunteer activities, only 21% of us seek out the activity or assignment on our own. We are more apt to be reactive than active.

- Most people who become involved want to do something useful and meaningful. Almost two thirds gave this response when asked why they first volunteered. (Source: 1988 *Independent Sector* study conducted by the Gallup Organization.)

The patterns of philanthropy are shifting. People are becoming involved in a greater variety of causes, and they are more concerned than ever before about how effective their charity is. They also want to be more involved in the organization's actual work and to follow what is done with their contribution, which means better accountability and clarity of purpose.

Today's contributors are more likely to want to experience their values in action. The stronger the conviction, the more the personal involvement; the more direct the contact, the larger the contribution or pledge. Although they may find it difficult to describe their feelings about why they volunteer, they clearly want to see that their actions make a difference. They gain something special from being needed and appreciated, and from extending themselves. Many speak of a spiritual satisfaction, an affirmation of what they hold dear. And all of these experiences are more likely to be found in volunteer activities, where there is one-to-one contact and personal service.

Volunteers tell me how giving has enriched their lives, enhanced their sense of self, and given special meaning to a stress-ridden existence. Recent studies by *Psychology Today, American Health,* and The Institute for Advancement of Health, have referred to a "helper's high." Social scientists and doctors are beginning to see how the human mind triggers special chemicals that enable us to feel more expansive, even euphoric. These chemicals, called endorphins, are released during esteem-building activities such as working to help others. The noted Harvard cardiologist and author Dr. Herbert Benson says that altruistic acts can produce a relaxation response equivalent to a deep state of rest.

To many who give, it's the spiritual reward that leads them to volunteer. For others, it's a belief that added blessings will be showered on those who help. For still others it is a simple recognition that we are our brothers' keepers. To millions, volunteering represents what is right with this world. An act of philanthropy *is* an act of love. In a world filled with violence, hatred, and suspicion, giving is an expression of faith, trust, and concern. Giving is spiritually uplifting—a powerful display of fundamental goodness.

Much of this book is inspired by the emerging body of knowledge about the health benefits that attend acts of giving and sharing. Over the past decade, some forward-thinking social scientists and medical experts have quantified the relationship between philanthropic activities and the physical and emotional well-being of people who engage in them.

While most people probably subscribe to the general theory that charity is "good for the soul," almost all would be hard-pressed to say why. Many would also be surprised to learn that philanthropic acts are also good for the mind and body. Research is beginning to confirm these claims. These emerging findings can transform the way people live and feel about themselves. For years, I have been one of a small group of people trying to show that philanthropy is a powerful emotional catalyst and protector of physical health—significantly more valuable to the well-being of mankind than was ever considered possible.

Thoughtful people have begun to speculate openly about the life-sustaining emotional, physical, and spiritual benefits generated by active giving. The early results of these inquiries confirm that philanthropic involvement is *measurably* wholesome for mind, body, and soul.

Could it be that the solution to America's troubles is found in its caring spirit? The thesis of this book underscores the answer: a resounding Yes. Giving can change America. Giving can also change your life—and the lives of everyone who inhabits this planet.

T · W · O

THE EXTRAORDINARY
BENEFITS OF GIVING

Living Longer and Living Healthier

There is a wonderful mythical law of nature that the
three things we crave most in life—happiness, freedom,
and peace of mind—are always attained by giving them
to someone else.

Peyton Conway March

Recent researchers who describe the extraordinary benefits that can come from giving include medical and social
scientists such as Allan Luks, Arthur White, T. George
Harris, Dr. Herbert Benson, Dr. Robert Ornstein, Dr.
David Sobel, Dr. Bernard Siegel, and organizations like
the Gallup Organization, *Prevention* magazine, the Roper
Organization, and *American Health* magazine.

Until his death, Norman Cousins led a pioneering project at UCLA to study the question of the mind's influence over the body. His most recent book, *Head First*,
is a dramatic confirmation of a line from Shakespeare:
"'Tis the mind that makes the body rich." Much of what
Cousins has discovered underlines the importance and
value of philanthropy.

Professor Mihaly Csikszentmihalyi of the University of
Chicago has for many years conducted a detailed inquiry
into the psychology of peak experiences. In his acclaimed
work *Flow: The Psychology of Peak Experience*, he exam-
ines emotional factors necessary for people to experience
the pleasurable, health-sustaining mental state he de-

scribes as "flow." His findings clarify the benefits of philanthropic behavior.

These new studies tell us that assisting others, through acts of charity or devotion to causes, improves our physical well-being. Giving is not just a minor influence on good health but the key to bodily and mental well-being. The studies show that for all ages (but particularly among the elderly), one way to escape premature physical and emotional deterioration is by staying active in the service of others.

For example, a ten-year study of the physical health and social activities of 2,700 men in Tecumseh, Michigan, found that those who did regular volunteer work had death rates two and one-half times lower than those who didn't. Those who serve others may be on a new path to longevity. Many noted philanthropists outlived most of their contemporaries—Ford, Rockefeller, Kroc, Mellon, Carnegie, McGaw, and Annenberg, to name just a few. And while their access to superior medical care undoubtedly helped them live longer, there is every reason to assume that their work on behalf of others also extended their lives.

Dr. Norman Vincent Peale tells of a study by a life insurance company of policyholders who lived to the age of one hundred years or older. One of the survey questions was: "What is the most important thing you have learned in your long life?" The most frequent answer was, "To love thy neighbor as thyself." Dr. Peale concludes: "They live longer . . . because they have freed themselves from deadly negative influences such as anger, hatred, suspicion, guilt, and anxiety." These toxic emotions can lead to cynicism, hostility and isolation, traits that Dr. Dean Ornish, noted heart specialist, identifies as major components of heart disease, high blood pressure, stroke, and probably cancer.

Norman Cousins and his UCLA School of Medicine task force studied the relationship between the mind and the immune system and found that emotional stress depresses that vital system, which can lead to chronic illness and death. Cousins hoped through his research to discover ways for the mind to send positive, health-sustaining messages to the immune system. These studies highlight the powerful role of the mind in repairing the body through stress reduction and the enhancement of positive emotions.

That the mind and body work together has been documented exhaustively. These scientists are trying to determine which thought processes and actions have a direct impact on the body. Not surprisingly, some consider concern for others the most important positive factor.

In another similar study, Harvard Doctors David Mc-Clelland and Carol Hirshnet discovered that people who watched a documentary about Mother Teresa's work with the dying showed an increase in immunoglobin-A, the body's first line of defense against viral infection. Other movies not focussed on compassion had no impact on the immune system. Dr. McClelland also found people strongly motivated by a drive for power to have lower levels of immunoglobin-A than people who were concerned for others. Dr. McClelland concludes: "This suggests that one way to avoid stress and illness associated with a strong power drive is to . . . turn the power drive into helping others."

In the effort to understand how the mind converts ideas and beliefs into biochemical realities, researchers have examined the relationship between social activities, work, and health. Norman Cousins's book describes in detail some ways in which the mind influences biology. A classic instance is the patient who rapidly recovers from a terminal illness after taking only a placebo—and, along with it, a belief in the curative powers of the "medication."

The mind can also reduce body temperature and strongly influence the immune system, including the production of "T" cells. A person's body often physically demonstrates his or her state of mind, so that a troubled mind will "produce" a troubled body. The link between body and emotions is dramatic indeed, and we are becoming more and more capable of predicting it.

Heart specialists like Dean Ornish and Dr. Herbert Benson, and cancer specialists like Dr. Bernard Siegel, all say that when we improve our relationships and emotional attitudes, we speed our recovery of health and reduce our risk of life-threatening illnesses. *Psychology Today* recently quoted Dr. Benson on the healing power of giving to others: "For millennia, people have been describing techniques on how to forget oneself, how to experience decreased metabolic rates, lower blood pressure, lower heart rates and other health benefits. Altruism works this way, just as do yoga, spirituality and meditation."

Dr. Dennis Jaffe in his book *Healing From Within* says, "Evidence is mounting that over-involvement with oneself, at the expense of the community, leads to psychological dislocation that results not only in anxiety but in various psychological ailments as well." As one medical researcher has broadly commented, "All disease is social in its origin."

The influence of religion has been documented in two studies of Mormons and Seventh-Day Adventists. Researchers found that the risk of cancer among active members of these groups was only about 50% as great as that of the average American, the risk of heart attack only 35%. Both groups frown on smoking, drinking, and overeating, but they also place great emphasis on practical charity. It may well be that the practice of brotherly love contributes to their members' greater life expectancy as much as their lifestyles.

When researchers in Israel ran a similar study on a group of Jerusalem residents, they found that those who described themselves as secular had a risk of heart attack four times greater than those who described themselves as religiously orthodox.

Dr. Redford Williams in *The Trusting Heart* reports similar results in Evans County, Georgia. Blood pressure levels were lower among residents who frequently attended church than among those who attended less often. Redford cites his colleague Dr. Berton Kaplan, who says that "many aspects of religious observance could be health enhancing and disease preventing. The world's major religions have as one of their core teachings the injunction to be less concerned with self and more concerned with loving others and treating them well."

The late Dr. Hans Selye has been called the father of stress reduction. Responsible for many early studies of the relationship between stress and illness, he coined the phrase "altruistic ego" to describe a person involved in philanthropic activities. "The love and gratitude we inspire in those we help . . . is a valuable payback," he wrote. "Like stress, love has a cumulative effect." This captures the essence of this book: sustained good deeds have a cumulative positive effect on our well-being.

A recent study of 188 companies by David Lewin of the Columbia Business School shows that employee morale was three times greater in companies with a high degree of community involvement than in companies that were uninvolved. Stress has long been a problem in the workplace, and corporate philanthropic activity may be a solution that has been a possibility all along.

Dr. Bernard Siegel in *Love, Medicine and Miracles* predicts an evolving course for the study of the link between altruism and illness: "There is a lack of grant money for research, but it will surely change as the psychology becomes more widely accepted. Research gradually improves medical care, and I believe that someday we will understand the physiological and psychological workings of love well enough to turn on its full force more reliably."

In a pioneering investigation of 1,500 women volunteers by sociologist Allen Luks, many subjects mentioned the enjoyable physical sensations they experienced while helping others and for some time afterward. Luks concluded that this "helper's high" reduces the emotional stress that interferes with the body's self-maintenance system. He went on to say, "These stresses cause the adrenal glands to release stress chemicals . . . that increase cholesterol levels that play a role in heart disease, raise blood sugar, and depress the immune system." In contrast, the women Luks investigated spoke of increased energy, a satisfying state of calm, and a feeling of warmth and well-being.

Researchers point to the endorphins, the body's own opiate system, as the source of the high people experience in doing good works. For some, these enhanced feelings last a long time. A number of volunteers claimed that since they had begun helping others they had experienced fewer stress-related ailments. In a nine-year study of relationships between social behavior and mortality rates of 7,000 Alameda County, California, residents, Drs. Lisa Berkman and S. Leonard Sym found that church members lived longer than those who did not belong to churches.

These emerging findings of the powerful benefits of philanthropic activity point chiefly to volunteers and face-to-face involvement. But there is a link with financial donations as well. When people give significant amounts of money, personal involvement usually follows—since interest, concern, and commitment accompany most gifts of money.

Instead of the old slogan "Give until it hurts," it seems we should say "Give until you feel great."

A New Path to Emotional Well-Being

God does not work in all hearts alike, but according to the preparation and sensitivity He finds in each.
Meister Eckhart

Struggling with inner conflict is never easy. Many people yearn for a more satisfying life, greater emotional balance, psychic well-being. And inner happiness and self-acceptance are difficult to achieve—and even more difficult to sustain. Life is full of disappointments, frustrations, monotony, difficulties at work, family and financial stresses. People become isolated and don't share life's joys easily with one another. As people get older, enthusiasm and satisfaction with life often diminish.

But there is one kind of experience that delivers emotional and psychic satisfaction time after time, day after day: helping other people. Volunteer efforts, charitable acts, generosity of spirit, and gestures of compassion all enrich and sustain our lives. Many of the 1,500 women studied by Allan Luks found that helping others took them out of themselves, gave them a greater sense of calm, reduced their anxiety levels, and left them with greater senses of self-worth.

Volunteering our resources and talents without thought of gain showers benefits on us we may never have expected. The "helper's high" can endure long after we are finished and can be recalled over and over again in memory. A stronger, better defined sense of self emerges through giving. Inner approval, feeling more positive about oneself—these are emotional benefits volunteers and donors cite in describing their feelings about acts of generosity. Older people particularly find volunteering helpful as they change and advance in years. The psychologist Eric Erickson says that altruistic behavior enriches what he calls the "integration phase" of a person's life cycle.

Some years ago I visited a man in his early nineties living in a Dallas, Texas, retirement home. His mind was as quick as an eighteen-year-old's, his movements as nimble as those of a man half his age. He had "retired" more then twenty-five years ago and ever since had volunteered as a student counselor at a nearby junior high school. He was still at the school every morning by eight A.M., and his attendance was perfect, sometimes counseling the children of parents he had helped twenty-five years ago. He gave to those youngsters every day, and in so doing heightened his own physical and mental health. Men who retire with no special plans often die within a year of retirement. But those like my friend from Dallas who find a way to share their lives with others seem to live on and on. And the longer they live, the more they have to share and enjoy.

In the Gallup survey of giving and volunteering, many of those interviewed sought emotional benefits, wanting to feel useful or needed. They enjoyed doing good works that contribute to an enhanced, more accepting self-image. They saw their service as a special connection or bond to others, seldom found elsewhere in their lives.

Volunteering and giving enhance self-acceptance. Emotional transference takes place during volunteer activity.

In giving love and concern to others we receive love, gratitude, and acceptance in return. The recently published book *Healthy Pleasures* puts it this way: "We can get a special kind of attention from those we help. This sincere gratitude can be very [emotionally] nourishing. Like the impoverishment of sensuality, we lack healthy doses of genuine appreciation and heartfelt thanks for our good actions. Most of us need such thanks from others, and need to feel that we matter to someone." It follows that the more we help others, the more we gain in self-appreciation and emotional well-being.

Dr. George Vaillant has monitored the progress of a group of Harvard graduates over a forty-year period and reported the resulting wealth of social behavior data in *Adaptation To Life*. He identifies altruism as one of the qualities that helps even the most poorly adjusted men in the study group to overcome stress and improve their lives.

In *The Broken Heart—The Medical Consequences of Loneliness*, Dr. James Lynch of the University of Maryland School of Medicine says, "'Love your neighbor as you love yourself' is not just a moral mandate. It's a physiological mandate. Caring is biological. One thing you get from caring is that you are not lonely, and the more connected you are to life, the healthier you are." Community and connectedness have long been acknowledged as important influences on mental health by the medical and psychiatric professions.

Dr. Dean Ornish, in *A Program for Reversing Heart Disease*, cites self-centeredness, the habitual use of the pronoun "I," and emotional isolation as destructive to emotional and physical health. People need good relationships with other people their whole life long. Newborn infants do not survive if they are not loved and nurtured, nor do the elderly. And even during our middle years, when we are most self-reliant, we are vulnerable. Giving and sharing not only help others, they also give us life.

Sharing and generous acts are "peak experiences" that can produce far-reaching psychic rewards. In the aforementioned 25-year inquiry into the psychology of optimal experiences, Professor Mihaly Csikszentmihalyi of the University of Chicago identified several conditions as essential to "flow":

- A sense of personal control over circumstances and events.
- A sense that one's skills are adequate to cope with the challenges at hand.
- A goal-directed, rule-bound action system.
- Solid feedback—clear clues as to how well one is performing.
- Intense concentration so there is no attention left over to think about anything irrelevant or worry about problems.
- The sense that time is distorted or stands still and self-consciousness disappears.

I think giving and sharing squarely meet all these criteria. Helping others provides guidelines, requires sensitivity and adaptive skills, sets goals in helping, and furnishes feedback through the gratitude of those who are helped. In volunteer work, the events are usually controlled by the giver, and the act of helping aids concentration and personal involvement. Volunteer work requires concentration on something beyond one's own problems, and when a volunteer helps another person—as soup kitchen volunteers know—time goes so fast that the day sometimes seems over when it has just begun.

To improve life and enhance self-worth, people need to improve their experiences. No one can buy happiness or contentment—they are not commodities. They emerge from what we do. Drinking, taking drugs, and overeating often lead to self-loathing and emotional and physical illnesses. Generosity and benevolence, on the other hand, lead to satisfaction and emotional and physical health. We all struggle with both constructive and destructive forces in our personalities. Acts of generosity enhance our feelings of self-worth, which in turn generate greater emotional harmony. A harmoniously ordered mind is the key to a deeper, richer, more enjoyable life.

To have a more balanced life, people need to increase their power to generate emotional rewards. Philanthropy and volunteer work are actions we can take right now to change the direction of our lives. In an age when personal control over circumstances is ever more difficult, an act of sharing gives us a way to direct and shape events. Recent studies with animals have shown that stress diminishes as the perception of being in control increases. Concentrated focus can produce a loss of self-consciousness and a reduction in tension and stress.

We feel good when our efforts succeed and we are thanked for our gift or help. This feeling of success comes to us in many ways. If the task is financial, a successful fund-raising effort can spur greater involvement and pride. Gratitude from those we assist can also be music to our ears. I suspect that Albert Schweitzer had a lot of positive appreciation as well as a mercifully strong physical constitution. I'm sure researchers could find many relationships between giving, gratitude, and inner harmony in the life of this dedicated Nobel Prize winner.

I remember the first campaign I conducted as a professional fund raiser, over twenty years ago. My client was

the Virginia Association of Realtors; the campaign's purpose, to endow a Chair of Real Estate at Virginia Com-
monwealth University in Richmond. The night before the
final results of the campaign were to be announced, we
were more than $100,000 short of our goal. The chairman
of the campaign, Alfred L. Blake, Jr., asked me if I thought
it would be out of line for him to announce the next day
that he personally would make up the difference and put
the campaign over the top. There was pride in his voice—
and tears in the eyes of the committee members—as he
spoke. I also remember the pleasure with which they
named the chair in honor of Mr. Blake's father, a pioneering real estate developer in Virginia. It was, for each of
those volunteers, one of the great affirming moments in
their lives. For Alfred Blake, it was one of his finest hours.

We all need appreciation, and the more driven among
us are often eager for approval. But many of us find little
sincere approval in our lives. Volunteer activity for the
benefit of others can lead to the sort of genuine approval
that benefits us emotionally while we help others. Most
Americans are people-oriented, and all of us enjoy having
people pay attention to what we say and do. Volunteer
effort fosters emotional well-being by empathetic acts,
building esteem, and putting our beliefs into practice. As
Csikszentmihalyi comments in *Flow: The Psychology of
Peak Experience,* "One cannot expect that everyone will
become involved in public goals. Some have to devote all
their attention just to survive in a hostile environment.
But life would be harsh indeed if people did not enjoy
investing psychic energy in common concerns, thereby
creating synergy in the social system."

We are made whole by making others whole. According
to Dr. Csikszentmihalyi, people who act out of concern
for others markedly improve their lives regardless of their
material circumstances. They lead more vigorous, bal-

anced lives, are committed to other people and the environment, are hardly ever bored, and cope well with whatever comes their way. They have structured their lives to benefit from a positive dynamic available to us all: What we do to help others increases self-appreciation and leads to a rich and rewarding life.

In his recent book *Power of the Plus Factor*, Dr. Norman Vincent Peale writes, "There is no doubt in my mind that people who care for other people and show that caring in loving unselfish ways most invariably have a strong deep current of the Plus Factor. What we are describing is a person who has discovered the key that unlocks the door to real happiness."

Dr. John Porter, a New York psychotherapist specializing in addiction, points out that "The amazing growth of self-help and recovery groups such as Alcoholics Anonymous, Overeaters Anonymous, and Narcotics Anonymous has largely come about because of the healing powers that operate when one individual or a group of people demonstrate a loving concern for others. When a recovering addict comes to the aid of a confused, desperate newcomer, the helper's self-esteem increases and then is further reinforced by the gratitude of the individual being aided. In essence, people heal each other in a loving and supportive environment. They give of themselves unselfishly and they form a strong bond with the other members of their recovery group. The result of this activity is a restoration to a wholesome and sane life."

Finding Spiritual Harmony

Great men are they who see that spiritual force is
stronger than any material force—that thoughts rule
the world.

Ralph Waldo Emerson

Religious belief is a powerful force in American life,
unifying, guiding, nourishing and giving meaning to the
lives of its followers.

Some 100 million Americans attend religious services
weekly. They contribute over $50 billion each year to
religious institutions.

It is impossible to discuss philanthropy without refer-
ence to religious convictions. Working in the field of
philanthropy for many years, I have learned about the
power of faith, conviction and belief. I'm convinced there
is a force, an energy, a spirit both in our own lives and
external to us that gives purpose to our days on earth. It
helps order the mind, bring inner harmony, shape our
highest aspirations. This spirit manifests itself in many
ways, but virtually all spirituality is grounded in two vital
principles: the need to do good for one another and the
need to love and respect each other.

In most religions the sanctity and value of one's neighbor is a paramount law. To preserve society and community, cooperation and brotherhood are essential. Religion
teaches us that it is noble and honorable to cherish and
sustain our brothers and sisters. For millions, religious
faith is the basis of life and actions are praiseworthy if
they grow out of a spiritual system of love and respect for
others.

Acts to help others have positive effects on our spiritual
well-being. Hundreds of people over the years have shared
with me the benefits they've derived from giving. In hum-
ble and eloquent detail they have described moments of

joy, peace of mind, satisfaction, and inner acceptance. When people give to their fellow man, something special happens. They are blessed with an extra dimension of inner harmony.

Philanthropy is a way of life for some people, dedicated benefactors who are spiritual to the core of their being. Bob Glaze of Dallas, Texas, stays active in business for only one reason: "So I can give more money away." C. Davis Weyerhauser of Tacoma, Washington, gives to more than two hundred charities every year because "This is my way of being a true steward of what God has entrusted to me." John and Donna Crean of Corona Del Mar, California, and Dick and Deanna Freeland of Fort Wayne, Indiana, give the most they can because they are grateful for what has been given to them. These people and many hundreds more like them give away millions every year—not out of obligation but as an expression of joy and well-being.

Of course, the spiritual benefits of giving are subjective and difficult to quantify. But this ambiguity is no different than the one faced every day by doctors and patients. When the doctor asks "How are you feeling?" the patient's answer is subjective, based on his or her feelings: "I feel fine," or "I feel worse today." In this interchange no precise measurements are made, but the doctor accepts the patient's assessment as valid. In psychology, these interchanges are more complex but essentially the same. The patient describes feelings or emotions in subjective terms: "I feel depressed," or "I feel like a new man." This is the "content" that an entire discipline uses to make diagnoses.

A few years ago a San Francisco psychiatrist and author, Gerald Jampolsky, opened a clinic to treat children and adults with terminal illnesses. He decided not to charge for his services but rather to trust that God would provide. The philosophy of his center is based on giving, not getting. He feels that his clinic gives new life to the principle that giving and receiving are, in truth, the same. As he says, "It's amazing how quickly our hearts open up to the presence of peace when we focus all our energy on helping a fellow traveler on the path."

When people tell me philanthropy has changed their lives, opened up new vistas, brought renewed compassion and love to their spirit, I believe what they say is true. However inarticulate a person's description may be, good deeds enlarge the heart and strengthen the soul. Spirituality and religion are forces that preserve the best in mankind. People aren't born with an abiding faith or peace of mind. They develop it in doing good deeds for others, acting to put their beliefs into practice.

A good deed, what the Torah calls *mitzvah*, connects us to the goodness of God, increases the righteousness in the world, decreases alienation and evil, helps our neighbor, enhances our self-appreciation, and makes everyone— ourselves included—richer.

T·H·R·E·E

EXPANDING YOUR
POTENTIAL FOR HAPPINESS

What the New Findings Suggest

The central purpose of each life should be to dilute the
misery in the world.

Karl Menninger

Bad news gets better press than good news, so I
wouldn't be surprised if you haven't heard the good news
about what helping others can do for you.

Drug addiction, for instance, is bad news that gets
millions of lines and thousands of hours of media
coverage. Government and organized medicine spend
hundreds of millions of dollars to investigate addictions.
Scientists, doctors, and therapists study the social and
medical issues involved and write countless books, articles, and research papers. Yet all this effort and attention
produce only limited results. Millions are also spent to
investigate and publicize other crises, ranging from toxic
waste to inflation and child abuse. These problems, too,
remain largely unsolved.

Altruistic activity is good news. A handful of researchers with limited funds are now showing that helping others can lead millions of people to improved health
and emotional well-being. But the media attention is min-
imal, the researchers have only token support, and the
public has yet to receive a comprehensive briefing on the
ways our lives can be positively transformed by giving and
sharing.

Even the nonprofit world has not realized the full potential of these studies. The $100 billion-plus American nonprofit sector has a "product" with healing qualities and needs to say so. These new findings have implications that can radically reshape and extend our expectations of life. If we demonstrate that giving and volunteering improve physical and emotional health, there will be a dramatic increase in philanthropy, with dramatic positive effects on givers and recipients alike.

Yet most organizations base their appeals on need, perhaps invoking the vague idea that giving and volunteering are "good for the soul" but offering little if any concrete evidence. For most, the idea that philanthropy is life-enhancing lies somewhere between a myth and a platitude.

Exactly what are the benefits of giving? They include:

Physical Benefits

- Greater longevity
- Significant reduction in toxic stress chemicals in the body (and so less stress)
- Enhanced functioning of the immune system
- Decreased metabolic rate
- Improved cardiovascular circulation
- Healthier sleep
- Help in maintaining good health

Emotional Benefits

- Increased self-acceptance
- Reduced self-absorption and sense of isolation

- Increased endorphin release (which provides a natural emotional "high")
- Expanded sense of control over one's life and circumstances
- Increased ability to cope with crises
- Stronger feelings of personal satisfaction
- Improved concentration and enjoyment of experiences
- Enhanced compassion, empathy, sensitivity to others
- Reduced inner stress and conflict

Spiritual Benefits

- Greater connectedness to God
- More receptivity to spiritual guidance
- Added involvement in charitable activity
- Heightened sense of appreciation and acceptance of others
- Sustained peace of mind
- Greater clarity about the meaning and purpose of life
- Enhanced quality of life

Considering how many people in our stress-ridden society are looking for physical well-being, emotional health and buoyancy, and spiritual harmony, there is every reason to believe they will become more involved in helping others if they are given the good news.

There seem to be virtually no negative effects to giving and volunteering. Research will likely establish that the more time, effort, and resources you give, the more benefits you will derive. There may even be a synergistic effect whereby the sum of your efforts is greater than its parts— where, in effect, $2 + 2 = 5$. Already there are people in philanthropy who attest to a synergistic effect among the large and fast-growing elderly in our society. Nor are the benefits to this group surprising when you consider how much they have to give—time, wisdom, sometimes money, and nearly always motivation to help others.

Americans have recently been changing their ways. Increase in physical exercise, shifts in eating habits, growth of counseling and psychotherapy, greater interest in meditation, and the proliferation of self-help programs are just a few of the signs that Americans are passionately interested in improving their physical and emotional well-being. Increased philanthropic activity can also be a life-affirming change.

The benefits of philanthropy are potential catalysts that can lead to a dramatic upswing in volunteering. With a strong benefit story, nonprofit organizations can tell their volunteers and donors about these new dividends, the "give-backs," if you will. Heightened awareness of the power of philanthropy will also broaden respect for giving.

The people whose needs are served by volunteers and donors will also benefit from increased involvement. More of them will receive more care, concern, and assistance than ever before. A new volunteer tutor might help an immigrant learn English; a local contractor might donate services and materials to help build a summer camp for inner-city Boy Scouts; a restaurant owner might donate food to a homeless shelter. I've seen countless success stories of such volunteer organizations as City Harvest of New York City, which helps restaurants and markets donate uneaten food to the hungry.

These are just a few of the changes that can occur if the benefits of philanthropy are made more widely known. Imagine an entire nation devoting at least five hours a week to philanthropic activity. What positive changes that would bring! The reduction in health insurance claims and lost working days alone would make the program worthwhile. The average American has about thirty-eight hours of optional time each week, so such a dream is far from impossible.

Then there are the indirect benefits of greater philanthropic involvement. People who feel good about themselves are more likely to be outgoing and charitable. Helping others is almost certain to bring about a shift in how we view them, making us more compassionate and tolerant. As our willingness to give and share grows, we will grow spiritually. When more people volunteer, the gaps left by reductions in government support for education and social and health services can be filled. And demand for health and counseling services should decline as people experience a greater sense of well-being.

Of course, most people do not change their lives easily, and many will hold back until the evidence about the benefits of philanthropy is overwhelming. If we are slow to give up smoking and overeating, I don't think we will stampede to do more good works.

But I'm betting it will happen. The nonprofit community can look forward to the day when more and more people come forward spontaneously to serve. And in serving others, they will discover that their lives have changed for the better

You Can Change By Helping Others

A bit of fragrance always clings to the hand that gives you roses.

Chinese Proverb

Some people have always understood the benefits of helping others and have led rewarding lives as a result.

One such person who has influenced me greatly is Dr. Arthur Frantzreb. Art has raised money for more causes than I can count, but does not call himself a fund raiser. He describes himself as a philanthropist. His work is not simply to encourage others to give money but to spread the message of each good cause he works for, planting seeds for its future work. Another person whose life as a philanthropist has influenced me is Milton Murray, who introduced the "Giving is Loving" calendars to the world. These calendars, with their daily philanthropic quotes, have touched the lives of thousands, including the President of the United States.

People active in philanthropy often have a limited view of what happens when they are urged to give to others. As I see it, the public's general appraisal when it is asked to help goes something like this:

- I'm asked to give time, talent, and other resources to a cause I feel I can support.
- I set aside time or resources, usually with some sacrifice.
- If my personal involvement with the cause is not very great, I don't really care how my efforts work out. To some extent, my actions are social and I'm filling time or just being with neighbors or friends. (This is especially true if I was motivated to give out of duty or guilt.)
- I have little expectation of anything more than a transient feeling of having done something of merit. (I expect to give without getting anything in return.)

This description seems dour, because it's missing the reciprocal benefits. People tend to view giving and volunteering as a one-way transaction, from givers or volunteers to recipients. For the giver or volunteer there may be some fleeting pleasures, minor satisfactions, a vague sense of redemption through good works. But few of them expect to receive an overflow of physical, psychological, and spiritual health from their activities.

People establish their perceptions of philanthropy early in life. They assign it value and seldom change their views. For a few, the acts of giving and volunteering are empowering, but for most there is little expectation of anything more than a token good feeling for a job done, a pledge honored, or one's word kept.

Philanthropy needs a definition that includes all the aspects of giving and sharing. So I offer here a new one that attempts to bring every part of the "philanthropic circle" into a coherent whole:

> Philanthropy is the mystical mingling of a joyful giver, an artful asker, and a grateful recipient.

All three—giver, asker, and recipient—benefit from the philanthropic experience. All three, the giver, the asker, and the recipient, are part of the philanthropic circle.

Until now, the call to help others has lacked an important element—proof that philanthropic activity enhances the giver's physical and emotional well-being. Now that evidence, that keystone, is being put into place. The new research delivers a clear and direct message: the more you give and share, the more you benefit.

At last we have concrete measurements of the return on investments of time and resources. These dividends are not material; they involve physical and emotional states that money cannot buy, qualities that enhance our lives. These benefits are easy to grasp, uncomplicated, and easy to predict. They function in a simple cause-and-effect manner—much like a family doctor's familiar counsel ("Follow a healthy diet, exercise regularly, reduce stress and you'll get better").

I wish the benefits of philanthropic involvement carried an unconditional guarantee. But, as with the doctor's advice, there's no sure thing or quick fix. *Consistent and frequent* involvement in giving and sharing can indeed transform people, but only if they follow sensible guidelines for living. The hyperactive, driven, overly competitive executive probably can't find much time in his schedule for more activity. So rather than devote many hours, he should give himself fully to one or two causes. It is his unique character and ability that count, not how many hours he gives. People need to give *who* they are, not just *what* they have.

To be with people, to be involved in a cooperative effort, to lose your self-awareness to a task or mission is my idea of how to truly benefit from giving and sharing. To quote Mother Teresa on volunteers, "I just ask them to come and love the people, to give their hands to serve them and their hearts to love them." The benefits of philanthropy are cumulative. They come from sustained efforts. You can't separate the benefits from the giving any more than you can attain them by pursuing them with no genuine concern for the cause.

Time has a great deal of value. Many people lead busy, involved, active lives. They have to operate on many levels: family, community, business, recreational, and social. Many are overcommitted and some lead very pressured lives. I know they are sorry they can't do more. Both husband and wife often work, and time together as a family is all the more valuable because it is difficult to find.

But the only way to take advantage of the benefits of sharing and giving is to find time and do it. You should consider setting aside time to become involved and committed to a cause that matters to you. I can hear you already: "But I just don't have the time." Consider the irony: you are striving for success and security in order to find physical, emotional, and spiritual well-being. Philanthropy can give you precisely what you're working for.

Limited vision is a barrier to a harmonious life. People can be so bedeviled by the demands of the moment that they can't order their own lives satisfactorily. The squeaky wheel gets the attention; the roar of ambition drowns out the impulse to set aside time to help others. Since the demands of society are continuous and always expanding, there are always many opportunities to help. So the rewards of philanthropy will wait patiently to be claimed.

Some people will postpone any effort to begin helping others until they have conquered the material world. But sometimes life seriously reduces people's options. They may find themselves overworked, overwhelmed, or in poor health. Sometimes a person who puts off sharing becomes the recipient of philanthropic services before he or she has ever tasted the fruits of giving. Many a homeless family in a shelter tonight never thought they would ever be on the receiving end of philanthropy. Ironically, the way back for many of them will involve giving one of the few things they now have—time. But time and money given earlier—and the joy such giving would have brought—might have been the turning point that kept a family from the ranks of the homeless.

I believe that the interest and participation in philanthropy will expand slowly, keeping pace with discoveries about the benefits to be derived from philanthropic involvement. I wish it could happen faster but until more people know about these discoveries, they will hesitate. Once the story gains momentum, though, I think it will grow and spread like a late summer grass fire fanned by a strong wind.

Of all the things that work against this good news, impatience—the desire for a "quick fix"—is the most dangerous. We expect immediate, almost magical results from our plans to change our lives. Sincere effort and dedication can produce remarkable results, but not overnight. We need to trust the process.

The qualities giving and sharing can deliver are the same ones most of America seeks. Giving offers you a new and better path with little in the way of sacrifice and a great deal to gain. This is a fresh new message. The more you give of yourself, the happier, healthier, and more contented you will become. Moreover, you will experience these benefits at the same time as you take your journey into sharing and giving. It is not a magic odyssey down a yellow brick road but a real world encounter promising enhanced health and emotional harmony. I'm convinced that if you use the techniques, guidelines, and approaches set forth in this book, you will have a much better chance of experiencing the complete range of benefits.

For some the promises have already come true. You have probably seen this in your own community. Some people radiate a special kind of well-being or spiritual harmony. One such quiet man of great kindness and dedication is Dr. Oliver Sacks, who tells of his efforts to help the mentally ill in the recent award-winning book and movie *Awakenings*. For years he had been caring for "lost souls"—men and women suffering from a destructive form of encephalitis. Many of his patients had been institutionalized for decades. They awakened his compassion, and in his book he describes how his caring led to a new personal tenderness and "awakening" to life. Those he treated for years became his teachers and friends. His is a powerful story of how philanthropy can change your life.

There are people like Dr. Sacks in your town. Look for these quiet philanthropists who are changing the world. When you find them, make a friend of them. They have much to teach you.

Maximizing Your Pleasures and Joys

We must not only give what we have; we must also give what we are.

Desire Mercier

Americans are beginning to realize that money and power alone don't produce happiness. Materialism will always be attractive, but growing numbers are moving toward a more spiritually centered life.

Every day I see people becoming more and more committed to causes that put their beliefs about the dignity of man and the best course for society into action. I see people becoming more willing to make things happen. I'm sure that part of this shift comes from a recognition that happiness cannot be attained passively. It requires energy and involvement. Philanthropic activity is a high road to enjoyment and happiness.

Few in our society ever attain great wealth, but those who do often display as much warmth, compassion, and wisdom as the rest of us. It is remarkable how many people who have amassed fortunes of a hundred million dollars or more set aside large portions for philanthropic purposes. They find great satisfaction in making a gift of millions to a favorite cause and seeing the good goals of that cause prosper.

Those of us with more limited resources gain the same measure of happiness when we share what we have.

Sometimes miracles do happen. I am reminded of a man in Richmond, Virginia, who gives away more money each year than he makes. (His salary is under $20,000.) When asked how he does it, he always says, "I just do it and it always works out okay." The very heart of philanthropy is commitment, willingness to support a cause for a long time with whatever resources you have. The greater your personal involvement, the greater the possibility of expanding your happiness and satisfaction.

We have all supported nonprofit organizations from a distance by pledging and probably also by volunteering. And I know my own experience is sharply enhanced when I see a project I have supported and am involved with blossom and succeed. The philosopher Viktor Frankel once said, ". . . Happiness can't be pursued, it must ensue . . . as an unintended side effect." I think we get closest to that unintended side effect when our service is wholehearted, regardless of our means.

A central theme of this book is how to make the most of the pleasures of giving and sharing. Most of us believe there is some benefit to compassionate acts, though the rewards may seem momentary and fleeting. But many don't experience the physical and emotional benefits from active involvement at all. I hope I can show them a path to joy and happiness. This path is not easy to describe, but it does exist.

Every organized religion teaches its followers that happiness comes in part from loving and serving our neighbor. Many philosophers have said that happiness comes from right actions, good deeds, and compassion—that our self-discovery, self-esteem, and fulfillment grow as we share with (and support) others. This has been the teaching of great men for centuries, from Moses and Buddha to Jesus and Mohammed. But in the absence of practical reasons to follow this wise counsel, its practical application in peoples' lives has been limited.

In industrial societies, many have come to believe that happiness is achieved through amassing wealth and power. In tribal societies, interdependence and sharing are seen as the essential aspects of survival—a happy person is one who contributes to the well-being of the group. Our new knowledge of the benefits of philanthropy can help bridge the gap between these two types of society. It can, indeed, contribute to mutual understanding and world peace.

Happiness is self-generated, something we set in motion for ourselves. Some of the best experiences in my life occurred when I stretched my talents and capacities to the limit trying to accomplish something for others. In particular I remember what my life was like before I was a giver—and what it is like today.

Some years ago my wife and I decided to stop talking about giving and become participants. The two of us each set aside $3,500 to set up the Lawson and Taylor Foundation. Neither of us had big money, and so the only way for this foundation to grow was for us to contribute to it each year.

We have contributed every year since then, and the results have been phenomenal. First, the foundation itself has grown to over $150,000, even though each year it gives away a healthy portion of its assets. Second, my wife and I have grown more spiritual in our outlook toward life and others, and in this new spirituality we have found peace of mind. And third, our incomes have grown each year since we set up the foundation, which has made it possible for us to give more away each year. An old expression I had never understood before has become part of our lives: "You can't outgive God."

The more we give, the more we have. Maybe that is what that "saint" in Richmond, Virginia, finds as he gives away more than he makes. We haven't come to that point yet, but the goal is one we may reach as our foundation continues to grow from our annual investments.And, naturally, I will give to the foundation as large a portion of the royalties from this book as the tax laws will allow.

I'm not one of those proselytizers who urges people to give away their wealth, abandon their families, and go to work among the sick and the destitute. I only suggest that since happiness comes from helping others, an investment of time, effort, and resources will probably lighten your burden and produce sustaining enjoyment. As the old axiom says, "The more you give, the more you get." Until now, many of us weren't sure just what we might look forward to getting. Scientists have given these uncertain dimensions some real definition.

All of us have an opportunity to increase our enjoyment of life while at the same time bringing benefits to others. The principle of giving to live asserts that if you increase your philanthropic activity, more benefits and rewards will come to you than to those you assist or the causes you champion. You have it in your power to test this formula any time you desire—if you are open to possibilities and willing to move along the Giving Path.

If you are skeptical, you might try the ninety-day "Give to Live Challenge." First go to your doctor and get a complete checkup. Ask him where you can take a simple battery of personality tests, and take them. Then get involved with your favorite cause—once or twice a week (say, 4-8 hours) for ninety days. When the ninety days are up, see your doctor again and revisit the testing counselor. Most important, *ask yourself* how you feel. I'd be willing to bet that you will see growth in self-appreciation, physical well-being, and spiritual harmony. Why not try it?

If the ninety-day challenge works for you, extend it to six months or a year. Set aside the time, develop a program and start experimenting with it. As Abraham Lincoln once observed, "Most people are about as happy as they make up their minds to be." What he didn't foresee was that real contentment and joy could come out of making up our minds to help others.

Dr. Robert Schuller, the pastor of the Crystal Cathedral in Garden Grove, California, said in his best-seller *The Be Happy Attitudes,* "We all know people who do not lie, kill, steal . . . [who] live a life of ease, comfort and noninvolvement. They appear to be kind and gentle and we are tempted to judge them to be 'loving people.' But real love is sacrificial commitment. If they take no daring risk, they're good—but for what." When Dr. Schuller asked psychologist Dr. Joyce Brothers what our deepest need was, she replied, ". . . human beings need love. It doesn't have to be the love between a man and woman. It can be love of mankind." Sharing and caring are primal human needs. And the life that fulfills these is beneficial to the giver and receiver alike.

The Leap of Faith

What shall I do with my life? How much am I willing to give of myself, of my time, of my love?

Eleanor Roosevelt

A growing body of evidence points to philanthropy as beneficial to people who give their time, energy, talent, and resources. This new evidence is more directional than conclusive. The early results I have shared with you are exciting and make a great deal of sense, but the whole story has yet to be told.

Beyond all the research, there lie your own philanthropic experiences. And those of other extraordinary individuals, people who have chosen to devote their lives to a cause. These people often radiate a passion, seem to have a richer sense of life.

I think of Paul Meyer, a founder of S.M.I. in Waco, Texas. He has made millions and each year gives millions away. He uses his considerable energy to make money, then takes that same energy and money and uses it to help others. What is amazing is that many people like Paul reach an age where infirmity would normally restrict them—without slowing down. They keep on giving, and even giving more year after year. Think of that ninety-year-old from Dallas who counsels junior high students.

These people have found something special. You can't help admiring them or wanting to be around them. Their positive energy is infectious, for they give everyone around them a new sense of the goodness of life. I see them often in my work, and they inspire me. They remind me how much a single person can do, how easy it is to change the world and change your own life. They are an amazing testimonial to the principle of giving to live.

In telling this story of the benefits of giving and sharing, I have presented a broad range of promising scientific inquiries and the stories of some wonderfully inspiring, dedicated people who give unselfishly and live longer and better lives as a result. Providing a backdrop to all of this is the collective wisdom of great philosophers who have consistently urged people to give of themselves, to fill their lives with good acts. Great rewards come to those who consistently care and share.

Do you believe that your participation in philanthropic activities can bring you greater well-being and a longer life? Are you convinced that there is more to philanthropy than meets the eye? Some of you may say, "Well, what you've presented makes sense, but I want proof positive. I want some more scientific evidence." Others may simply not believe, or may suspect that these powers of philanthropy can enrich everyone *except* themselves.

Well, you will never know unless you try. Are you willing to take that proverbial leap of faith with only limited evidence? Can you set aside your fears and make the practice of giving more central in your life? Are you willing to act—and trust that positive results will follow?

One way to begin: Ask yourself how important these new benefits might be to you. What are you willing to do to live longer, to feel better physically and emotionally? Most of us value these ends highly enough that we will not simply reject them out of hand. So if you look carefully at what I'm proposing, you may conclude that the risks are well worth the potential benefits. Consider giving a few hours a week, donating money or resources, getting involved in a cause. The "tenfold increase" mentioned in the Bible may arrive in the form of health, emotional well-being and spiritual harmony. There are no guarantees, but what else has brought you these dividends recently?

I am not trying to trick anyone into doing anything. I truly believe in the powers of philanthropy and I hope to both inform and inspire you. The new research on giving has tremendous ramifications. How meaningful this approach to living can be in your own life is entirely up to you. It might cut into some of your social time, your television time, or your fishing time. It is a rare person, however, who can't free up a few hours a week for volunteer work.

Most of us spontaneously help friends and neighbors. What I'm suggesting is involvement in the world of philanthropy: working with a church group to feed and house homeless people, teaching youngsters how to swim, or raising funds for a senior citizens' center. There is no lack of opportunity.

Another way to get a feel for what participation can mean is to spend a little time talking to people who have been touched by the powers of philanthropy. Pick a non-profit organization and ask the director to introduce you to one of their volunteers or donors. Sit down with this person and ask him or her to tell you what giving and volunteering has done for them. And when you get home, drop me a letter and let me know what they said. Send your letters to:

Douglas M. Lawson
545 Madison Avenue
New York, NY 10022

I will use your stories in my research; and you can use their stories in your own life-changing decisions.

I'm old enough and experienced enough to know that this message is at odds with powerful forces in our society. In this age of self-interest it isn't easy to capture the attention of the millions scrambling for wealth, prestige, and power. Achievement, material gain, and security are drives as ancient—and as seductive—as our concern for one another. Thousands of years ago, charitable acts were also locked in conflict with the desire for wealth and power. But at the dawn of civilization people possessed no scientific evidence that supported the physical, psychological, and spiritual benefits of philanthropic acts. Yet even in those early days people instinctively knew that being a benefactor had magical qualities. The Torah, the works of Jesus, the teachings of Plato and Mohammed all invest philanthropic activity with a special grace—a grace that needs to be rediscovered in every generation.

People, as a rule, don't like change. We develop daily

rhythms, structure our activities, and resist change. Change brings stress and dislocation. Even when faced with evidence that changes need to be made, we balk. Ask any doctor about the difficulties they have in getting their patients to quit smoking or cut down on fats in their diet. Too many of us ignore or resist good counsel until we find ourselves in life-threatening situations. The medical evidence is all but conclusive, and still we ignore it. We will doubtless do the same with our new knowledge about philanthropy. Only time will tell. People will not easily alter their perceptions of giving.

Some who give their time, talent, and treasure don't get much pleasure and satisfaction from their benevolence. Perhaps their involvement has become automatic rather than personal. Some people refer to their volunteer efforts as sacrificial, and some activities lose their energy and appeal over time.

It doesn't have to be this way. I will later describe approaches anyone can adopt to reduce or eliminate this malaise, which some call emotional fatigue or burnout. Renewal can occur, and the remedies to burnout are practical and sensible.

While there are no known disadvantages to increased giving except overextension, the benefits won't be visited upon you overnight. Most likely they will blossom as you deepen your resolve, increase your involvement, and change your perceptions. Philanthropic activities don't provide a quick fix for a life badly out of balance. But acts of sharing and caring nourish the giver.

I can't tell you how long it will take or how quickly you will experience these powers of philanthropy, but I'm convinced that it will happen. You may need a "leap of faith" in the beginning, but all the elements needed to produce a small miracle in your life are already in place. To begin, you need only believe it can be so and start.

Why not take the ninety-day "Give to Live Challenge" now? And when the ninety days are up, drop me a line and let me know how you feel about your life. You just might be amazed.

F · O · U · R

GETTING INVOLVED

Matching Your Talents to the Opportunities

Each citizen should plan his part in the community according to his individual gifts.

Plato

You *personally* can make a difference. Your community needs your gifts of money, but it also needs your time and your special skills. Many people take the first opportunity that comes along to volunteer. But it makes more sense to work at what you do best. If you do, you will be happier and you will make more of an impact.

The kind of organization you support is important. Each of us is unique, so different causes will appeal to different people. And since there are more than 800,000 nonprofit organizations in America to choose from, there is bound to be one for you. If one cause doesn't strike a responsive emotional chord, if you don't feel some natural pull, then pass it by. You may feel you ought to volunteer for a given cause simply because you were asked to, but this sort of half-hearted commitment may dilute your time and resources and lead you to give less to an activity that really means a lot to you. Extra energy and emotional dividends will come from a solid commitment to a course you believe in.

Most people give at least some of their time and money to their own religious institution, and if you are looking for an opportunity to volunteer, this would be a good place to start. Most denominations provide a wealth of services to many kinds of people and for many needs. Yours might have local programs to feed or shelter the homeless, aid international famine relief, offer legal assistance to the poor or support for the arts, work to improve the environment, care for preschool children, or provide meals and activities for the elderly—and many, many more. You can easily find out about programs your denomination offers by getting in touch with its regional office. And such work often leads to positions of responsibility and leadership.

There usually isn't a single clearing house in a community for people interested in volunteer work, so a person who wants to volunteer needs to be inquisitive and persistent. The United Way is another good place to begin in your community. There you can find out about local service opportunities in its many participating organizations.

What skills do you have? Probably more than you think. Take a minute and write down what you feel you do best. Your goal is to be comfortable and satisfied with your volunteer work and to have a sense of mastery over your task, even if it's as simple as stuffing envelopes. When people know they can do a job, they are less likely to feel threatened or disheartened. As you make this inventory, assess your skills in:

- teaching and instructing
- persuasion and sales
- administration and clerical work
- counselling and guidance
- socializing and entertaining
- analysis and writing
- creative and artistic work
- logistics and organization
- construction, repair and crafts
- public speaking and advocacy
- physical assistance and caretaking.

After all, if you have a clear idea of what you can do and enjoy doing, the choice you make is more likely to be suited to your skills and interests. If you have poor organizational skills, let someone else organize the charity dance. If you have flat feet or knee trouble, don't volunteer as a sidewalk Santa. But if you are good at balancing a checkbook, you might enjoy doing the accounting for a charity marathon. If you are good at listening and hugging, consider volunteering to visit a nursing home.

Most people have pretty good instincts about what activities fit their talents and interests. When a poor possibility is presented to you, some emotional response— probably your blood pressure—will signal if it's a misfit. Listen to these internal signals and take on only the tasks that feel right. If one doesn't seem comfortable or doable, say no and wait for the next opportunity

Many people feel that the four or five hours they can give each week are not worth the self-analysis and detailed planning I am recommending. But I believe such effort will make your volunteer time and giving much, much more pleasurable and effective. Commitment and a good match are the beginning of good service. You can take control of your own volunteer time and turn it into an adventure. There's no better time to start than now.

Getting Started, Doing More—A New Approach

Do all the good you can,
By all the means you can,
In all the ways you can,
In all the places you can,
At all the times you can,
To all the people you can,
As long as you ever can.

John Wesley

Most Americans give both money and time for others. *Independent Sector* says 67% of adults volunteer time each year, averaging four hours a week. The typical American household gives $740 a year to charity. I am sure that most Americans have volunteered or given money at some point in life, often with great satisfaction.

But sometimes the experience of giving is tedious or even unpleasant. As one disgruntled volunteer said to me, "What's the use in complaining? My intentions were good, but the situation wasn't. I felt like a misfit." One especially energetic volunteer told me her troubles in trying work with orphanage babies. She applied, had her background checked, spent four nights in class learning to care for the infants, and only then was told there were no volunteer openings for a year. One dedicated volunteer told me how he doggedly raised money even though he hated making cold-canvass calls.

Incidents like these wound the spirit. People don't say much about them because they mistakenly believe giving and volunteering are *supposed* to be unpleasant and sacrificial. The recipients benefit, to be sure. But for the volunteer it is just work, "giving up" something in order to be of service. Although this is a fairly common attitude, it is dead wrong. Acts of giving and sharing need not be unpleasant.

Many people in philanthropic work are miscast. We often commit ourselves to service before considering whether or not the job fits us. Out of a sense of duty we show up and work at tasks we dislike. I don't claim that every moment of volunteer activity should be a peak experience, but there are steps you can take to choose the right area of service for you and improve your experience of volunteer work.

The first is to find out who you are and how you feel about service. Ask yourself these questions:

- How well do you get along with people?
- Do you work well around demanding people? In tense situations?
- Do you prefer structured or unstructured work?
- Do you like selling, soliciting, or negotiating? Are you comfortable asking people for support, money, or assistance?
- Do you need frequent or immediate feedback, or do you work well with little or no recognition?
- Do you work best when you direct your own efforts, or when others are in charge?
- Do you enjoy doing work you know you can do, or do you enjoy stretching your limits?
- Are you drawn to difficult or seemingly impossible causes?
- What projects do you remember that you loved, where you "lost yourself?"
- List ten activities you know or think you would enjoy.

Be honest about yourself, and pick work that fits *you*. Believe me, it's out there. I think that most unhappiness among volunteers comes from taking on work that doesn't fit their character and emotional needs. If you don't like asking strangers for money, don't do it. There are many, many other ways to help. It's important to know or sense what fits you. Dr. Hans Selye says, "Much of the trouble people have comes from their trying to be something they are not."

When you give or volunteer it's important to enjoy the experience—not necessarily every moment, but many of the moments. The quality of your volunteer experiences will determine the physical, psychological, and spiritual benefits you receive from sharing. If you are at odds with your assignment or struggling with personality clashes, all you'll receive from your giving is more stress, not harmony and well-being.

It's easy to see how stressful situations can arise. When people admire the work of an organization, they gladly volunteer. Many will say, in effect, "I'll do whatever I'm asked. So many people volunteer, you have to take what they give you." Others will assume they don't have the right to ask for a special assignment, lest they be labeled demanding or difficult.

Yet active pursuit of the right kind of work for you is the only approach that makes sense. You can't experience the rewards of giving if you're trapped in a boring, irritating, or unsatisfying assignment. If it seemed right at first but then turned wrong for you, ease your way out of it. It's essential that you gain satisfaction and joy from your volunteer time.

Negative voices about volunteering are strong: "Get real—most volunteer work is just plain boring." "The organization I support doesn't have interesting jobs." "If you think you can enjoy this, you're living in a dream world!"

If you are hearing these voices, I suggest two ways to change your experience:

- Look for a cause where your needs are more likely to be met. There are thousands. Find out about other organizations and their needs and projects.
- Stay with your current cause, but create an assignment for yourself that fits you. Find a change of pace.

The benefits that can come from supporting a cause you believe in are extraordinary. But you won't experience them unless you take your own needs into account and aim for enjoyable experiences in all your giving. You can maximize your opportunities if you keep in mind Dr.

Csikszentmihalyi's conditions for peak experiences. Pick a task

- that you are capable of doing.
- that has clear goals and structures.
- that provides immediate feedback.
- where you can exercise some control over circumstances.
- where involvement becomes effortless and you feel absorbed, where your self-consciousness disappears.
- where time passes quickly and pleasurably.

Greater satisfaction is also possible in giving money. Investigate the cause you are interested in—call the people in charge. Visit them. Find out more about their needs. Earmark your funds for a particular project and follow its progress. Get to know other volunteers in the organization. Find out about other needs—perhaps you have special contacts or resources they can use. When you become personally involved in your giving, you can change the arms-length to an arms-around approach.

Barriers to Involvement

> It is one of the most beautiful compensations of this life that no man can sincerely try to help another without helping himself.
> *Ralph Waldo Emerson*

People offer many reasons for not becoming involved in service and giving—particularly shyness, lack of time, or infirmity. These reasons are sometimes real, sometimes excuses.

Many people, especially busy young professionals, schedule their lives so that there is hardly an unfilled moment in the day. For older people physical weakness, illness, and limited energy are real problems. Women with families, especially working mothers, have so many demands on their time that they could use a 28-hour day just to take care of the work they already have. Lack of spare time (and energy) puts a real limit on what they can offer.

But there are ways to make opportunities for service in a busy life. Look at your schedule and put your current commitments to a couple of simple tests: give yourself a "Value Scale Review." What you're are trying to do is free up a few hours a week for volunteer service.

First, let the roaring sound of words like "impossible," "out of the question," and "you must be crazy" die away. You need to have an open mind to explore new alternatives.

Next, list the major blocks of time in your typical work day and days off: what you have to do, and what you can change. Probably, your days off will have more flexible time. Give each activity—work, housework, recreation, exercise, sleep, social events—a value rating from 1 to 5, with 5 being most valuable. Among the 1, 2 or 3 ratings is a possible opportunity for volunteer time. Choose an activity you can most easily change.

Third, select a type of service that interests you. Ignore for the moment the specifics and concentrate on the ideal type for you. Give that service a value rating of 4 and compare it to the activity you selected as easiest to replace. Since much of our workaday life is repetitive, this block of "spare" time will likely be pretty consistent from week to week. After reflection, you might find that you do have a regular time for volunteer service after all.

A simpler approach is the Active/Passive test. Watching

TV is passive. Feeding the children is active. Your passive activities are more easily available for volunteer service time, but even active activities can be made available. Maybe the children, if they are old enough, can prepare one meal a week themselves, freeing you up for a few hours.

Most people would gladly give many hours to save a dying child without worrying much about the displacement of other things in their lives. But most causes don't have this kind of urgency, and so they seem less important. And sometimes we really need private and family times to stay sane, or an extra job to pull us through financially. Illness and infirmity are real. Still, some of our time can be rearranged.

Let's look at some of the ways people deal with thoughts that are barriers to involvement.

"I Don't Have Any Special Talents"

This is so often heard and so seldom true. Spending friendly time with older people or helping blind children require only love and sensitivity. Most volunteer work is easily learned. Think first of the type of service that interests you and you are sure to find tasks you can already do. The woman who founded Mothers Against Drunk Driving (MADD) says she began the organization without any knowledge at all of how to do it. She just did what needed to be done as it came up, and learned the ropes as the movement grew.

"I'm Shy and Have Trouble Meeting People"

Deep down, many of us are shy. Shyness is natural and very human. So are spontaneous friendliness, acceptance, and appreciation among volunteers and those we help. There is apt to be a real sense of community and love among volunteers that will embrace you once you take the plunge. Your shyness will diminish if you face your fears, and the world of service is a receptive place. When you help someone in need, your shyness often just fades away.

"I'm a Person with Only Limited Resources"

Most people don't have much money to spare. Some people pledge an amount and then get a small part-time job or do craft work to meet their goal. Teenagers do neighborhood chores and give what they earn. Theater groups stage plays and donate the proceeds. Your resources are limited only by your imagination. To paraphrase the Bible, where your commitment is, there will your heart be also.

"There is No Particular Cause That Interests Me"

Strangely, people sometimes feel this way because they aren't involved enough. If you only give occasional efforts or stay on the sidelines of a group, you won't get a solid feel for service. You need to come closer to the center and feel the warmth. Grassroots activity is sometimes the answer. I know a man who was on the board of an overseas relief agency. He found the board meetings dull, dry, and boring, so he left his prestigious post and began serving as an unpaid sales representative promoting the crafts of the foreign communities served by the agency. This simple sales transaction provided him with a more direct sense of helping and much more personal satisfaction.

"My Charity Begins at Home"

This usually means that our family needs all we can give
and do. Sometimes it is just a humorous admission that
finances are tight. And service *should* begin at home. The
first place to give our energy and love is to those we love
the most. And sometimes our family has urgent needs we
simply must address. But outside service can also soften
our hearts and lead us to greater sensitivity. We can return
home with a renewed love for our families that can help
transform a dysfunctional home into a place of warmth
and mutual respect. Once your heart has been expanded
to include others, your own immediate family will also
receive your renewed compassion and giving. Dr. Tessa
Warschaw in her book *Rich is Better* says, "I have met
many . . . successful men and women but none of them
have been truly filled up with anything but their relationships, the love that they give. I have never met anyone
with money but with no generosity from the heart who
has been happy."

Pacing Yourself—Easy Does It

> Seek always to do some good somewhere. You must
> give some time to your fellow man. For remember, you
> don't live in a world all your own.
>
> *Albert Schweitzer*

Another reason many volunteers and benefactors are
not satisfied in their giving is that they overextend themselves. While devoting yourself heroically to a cause may
be admirable, it can also be self-defeating. Too often we
think that what is worth doing is worth overdoing. This

may be good for the organization you've chosen, but it isn't good for you. Why? Because driving yourself beyond a sensible limit can lead to disillusionment, resentment, and burnout. I have seen this happen over and over. A person will set out with great optimism, promise more than can be delivered, and then, feeling trapped, push to the limit. The resulting stress *always* leads to setbacks and dissatisfaction.

Every volunteer should carry a card with five small phrases on it:

- Don't overextend yourself.
- Don't overpromise.
- Don't try to do it alone.
- Don't overreact.
- *Do* find time to enjoy your work.

Too many people drop away because they don't know how to pace themselves. One bad experience can lead to a negative attitude toward volunteerism that can last for a lifetime. The best counsel I know is "Take small bites." Start slow, be aware of your energy level, and take your time.

Try to see volunteering as an opportunity to find enjoyment and pleasure through sharing. By helping others you enhance your self-image and match your skills to real needs that otherwise might not be met. If these elements are missing, reconsider your commitment. Don't be a martyr. Giving until you drop can only lead to frustration, certainly not to a dynamic, fulfilled life. Slow down, enjoy the journey, and let the experience of giving gradually fill your life with joy.

Of course, reality always turns out differently than we imagine when we enlist in our chosen cause. And even when our volunteer work is going well, our family and career often demand our attention. When this happens, protect yourself. Back away from your volunteer work until you meet your more basic commitments. It is absolutely appropriate to step back when family or work crises arise, just as it's sensible to step back from an unsatisfactory volunteer task. There is no loss of personal integrity in such a move. Your goal is both to advance the cause you believe in and to enhance your life. You cannot do either if you are overcommitted.

Volunteers who serve for many years learn to moderate their efforts. They seek opportunities that match their talents. They seek out the tasks that seem sweetest to them, take their time, become comfortable with their assignments, and then do the best they can. This benefits both them and their cause.

Most volunteer, fund-raising, and advocacy activities require teamwork. Seldom do two people approach the same project in the same way. Some cooperate easily, while others challenge authority. There is always some friction in the volunteer ranks, and I am convinced that this energy helps the total effort. But acceptance of others, tolerance, and patience always enrich the experience. The lack of these qualities can sabotage a project and make the work unpleasant for all. If you find yourself in this kind of situation, again, the best thing to do might be to look for a volunteer task more suited to your needs.

Many people are intensely loyal and have strong emotional ties to their causes and the institutions that promote them. For some, their charitable organization is almost an extended family. Their respect and dedication to the organization's goals is unswerving even through hard times.

But for others, commitments that were once fresh can become burdensome drudgery. These people often stay involved out of pride or closeness to a cause they once held dear. But people change, and so do their energies and circumstances. If you feel restless, stale, unhappy with different leadership, look for a new challenge. Start first within the organization. But if you don't find it there, bring your involvement to a close with grace and thanks for what you have received, and look elsewhere.

Once they have gotten into the swing of volunteering, most people find a number of organizations they admire and would like to help. A new kind of service can be reinvigorating and exciting. Change and challenge keep all of us flexible and involved. This is not desertion. Rather it is a celebration of your healthy respect for the quality of your own life.

It is important that you find satisfaction and real meaning in your volunteer efforts and giving. They are the key to finding the rewards of philanthropy. Try to follow the advice of Leo Buscaglia in his book *Loving Each Other*: "Joy, humor, laughter—all are wonderful, easily accessible tools for bringing comfort. . . . When we feel joyful, euphoric, happy, we are more open to life, more capable of seeing things clearly and handling daily tensions."

Enlisting the Entire Family

It is a rare and a high privilege to be in a position to help people understand the difference that they can make not only in their own lives but in the lives of others by simple giving of themselves.

Helen Boosalis

Each single volunteer, each single donor, each single advocate is a powerful resource, possessing extraordinary powers. Becoming a giver can lead to greater personal harmony and also to greater involvement on the part of your family. By enlisting them in your sharing, you double, triple, or quadruple your contribution to the cause you value.

Perhaps the most successful effort in the history of Religion in American Life was the "Invite a Friend" campaign to motivate more Americans to attend religious services. For every successful formal solicitation of wealth from a great benefactor or foundation, there are tens of thousands of effective requests from friends and relatives. The great philanthropic work of America is built on local person-to-person effort, and every donor and every volunteer counts. A committed volunteer can motivate family and friends, widening the circle of the cause he cares about and expanding the benefits of sharing.

I have often seen entire families work together for a cause, particularly at religious events. I am sure this is tied to lessons learned in religious practice. The religious cause benefits mightily from this kind of wholesome response, and the families grow in solidarity as well.

When you are considering giving to or joining a cause, why not consult the whole family? Deciding together what to support can have a wonderful effect on family harmony. And working on a cause by parents and children together is a wonderful form of family communion, creating a closer bond of love. Collective ties like this are healing, especially in our society in which so many factors weaken family relationships. Truly, the family that gives together grows together.

Sharing the experience of giving is also a way to show children the value of respect and love for others. What better model can a child have than parents who make sharing with others an important part of their lives? A parent who actively works for important values introduces children to a world where they can make a difference and experience the friendship and gratitude of others. A par-

ent's selfless service helps children understand the value
of service for others and gives reality to the biblical injunction, "It is better to give than to receive."

Family volunteering also helps children build a positive
sense of self as they grow. Young children are highly
impressionable, learning quickly from the world around
them. What their parents do never goes unnoticed and
seldom goes unimitated. Teaching children generosity of
spirit by including them in family philanthropy can have
far-reaching positive effects on a child's character, setting
them up for a richer and more harmonious life.

By including your children in your giving, you are helping them to a second path of knowledge that can teach
them what formal education cannot. The path of sharing
and giving is a path of wisdom and involvement with
others. While you prepare them for college, career, and a
family, give them the gift of giving. It will help them reach
a state of well-being that comes from a love of others
together with a proper love of self.

There is a tender trap in this recommendation. The
best teaching for children is *doing*. If you include your
children from their earliest ages in your acts of sharing,
they will learn the lessons of compassion, cooperation,
and dedication to good causes. And working together
with them will bind your hearts together.

For two specific groups of family members the act of
sharing is critical. For the very young, learning to be
compassionate, sharing, and responsible is essential to
their becoming healthy and joyful adults. For the elderly,
sharing helps develop a stronger life force, decreases depression and lethargy, and banishes loneliness. Pastoral,
medical, and counselling experts all advise older people
that sharing their time with others helps avoid isolation
and generates self-esteem and respect.

So enlist your family in your sharing. You will be giving
them gifts of incalculable value.

F · I · V · E

ALL AGES CAN GIVE

Early Lessons

The heart of the giver makes the gift dear and precious.
Martin Luther

Modern medical and social sciences agree that a person's patterns of generosity are formed during the first four or five years of life. The parents' example is especially important in determining whether or not a child becomes a person who shares easily. According to Dr. Lee Salk, the way parents and other close relatives behave, what they teach, and how they treat others all set the stage for a child's life as a giving person.

My years of work with religious, academic, cultural, and social welfare groups have given me some insight into what helps people grow into healthy, compassionate adults. I would stress these points on childhood development:

- Childhood experience and training are critical influences on patterns of giving.
- Parents should provide a variety of giving experiences for their children. By doing so they contribute mightily to their children's chances of becoming sensitive and giving adults.
- Little children are naturally self-centered. It is up to the parents to introduce the child to a give-and-share lifestyle.
- By the age of three, children understand that other people are different, and can begin to identify and empathize with the complex emotions of others.

- Money and how it is valued are important in early childhood development. When families are insecure about money, that insecurity persists in the child, who as an adult will often develop an obsession with making money.
- Both word and example are important in teaching children to be generous and caring. If parents encourage sharing verbally but act selfishly, the child will be confused. How can a child learn sharing hands and an open heart from miserly parents?
- Sharing is best taught in a child's own terms: "Helping another person makes *you* happy."
- Parents should encourage small children to act on their own impulses to share. These first spontaneous acts of charity give form and meaning to the child's own experience.

When I was very young I remember my father suggesting I share my candy, toys, and a few pennies. His approval and praise made me glow with pride, and gave me a positive attitude toward giving. I see now that my father was helping me form an image of myself as a sharing person.

A daughter of the Rockefellers told a gathering on National Philanthropy Day in New York City that her father gave her an allowance of 15 cents a week. He had her make up three boxes: "mine," "savings," and "others." Each week she put one nickel in each box. At Christmastime, she and her father emptied the "others" box and counted it. After much discussion with her father she selected a charity, went to the bank with her father, got a cashier's check for the amount in the box, and mailed it to the charity. She proudly proclaimed that she still followed her father's principle of "one third to charity."

Giving, sharing, and volunteering involve a complex set

of value judgments and motives. Our willingness to help others doesn't spring from a genetic matrix alone. Some recent studies of the roots of childhood sharing and compassion prove to be revealing. Young children cannot easily express their own motives, but two- and three-year-old children can be seen in these studies to share spontaneously with each other. Unfortunately, these children have not been tracked (as they grow up) to see if they develop altruistic personalities, but I think it is reasonable to conclude that early givers are lifetime givers. Early misers are lifetime misers—except for Scrooge, who is a product of Dickens's imagination.

I recently saw a three-year-old child of a friend of mine watch two seven-year-old children eat some candy. The older children saw the three-year-old staring at them and offered him some of their candy. The three-year-old's immediate response was to offer them some of the potato chips he was eating from a bag held by his father. The whole incident was quite spontaneous and told me a lot about the future character of all three children. But add one fact to this scene, and you see how children can teach us: the older children were African-American and the three-year-old was white.

Dr. Bruce Baldwin, a behaviorist, suggests that parents should consider the following ways to teach social responsibility:

- Discuss the values and benefits of sharing and participation with your children. As they grow in understanding, introduce more and more information about these good values.
- Teach your children to help in community and church projects.
- Don't insulate your children from the harsher realities of life. Visit missions, hospitals, homes for the

elderly, and poor neighborhoods together to see first-hand the need for sharing.

- Teach your children how to give part of their allowance to a cause that appeals to them.

We give double messages to our young people. On the one hand we encourage them to make money, to be the best, win it all, take charge, work hard, never give up on the American dream. On the other hand we try to give them a sense of responsibility to others and a sharing heart. It seems that society considers sharing and giving of secondary importance during the climb to success. Even sadder, many people equate empathy for others with weakness.

Our society isn't perfect and never will be. But it would improve if we were to put less emphasis on "making it" and "getting my share of the pie." I don't hear much about "*giving* my share of the pie." Many see acts of generosity as something to postpone until the big slice of the pie has been won, and until then most energy, effort, and concern stays fixed on the race for material success. Some upwardly mobile young Americans seem to worship power, position, and money. It's not the race I mind so much as their singleminded devotion to it, their lack of balance, and the limited energy and resources they make available for community sharing.

Many who work hard to achieve the material dream will pass on their concentrated, frantic devotion to their children. Children are great mimics who readily absorb and reflect their parent's behavior; this driven existence is powerfully attractive. If just 5% of this energy could be harnessed to help our social and educational problems, it would make a tremendous impact. And once harnessed, these people would begin to discover their capacity for compassionate and empathetic community leadership.

Recently, according to a *New York Times* story, a group

of seven-year-olds in Trumbull, Connecticut, were told about the plight of homeless children. The results were astounding—and yet they were, for children around the world, quite ordinary. Elizabeth gave $1 from her savings earmarked for a Samantha doll and a present for her brother. Guy Lev gave 80 cents he had been saving for a new Nintendo magazine. His only comment? "People are more important than magazines." Caroline Tanski gave the $10 her grandmother had given her for her eighth birthday. In ten days these and other children in their school collected $468.59 for the homeless. What a lesson in giving for all of us who call ourselves "adults."

America's young people are within the force fields of the electronic media, advertisers, and schools. These can and in some ways do contribute to their formation in generosity. Advertisers especially can show children giving and sharing while the product is being promoted. And children's television shows and books can be produced with themes of generosity and compassion. Religious organizations and groups like the Boy Scouts, the Girl Scouts, Boys and Girls Clubs, 4H Clubs, YMCA/YWCA and other groups for young people have great opportunities to teach a life based on sharing. But the greatest opportunity is right at home, with your own children.

Sweet Bird of Youth

> People can be divided into three groups: those who make things happen, those who watch things happen, and those who wonder what happened.
>
> *Nicholas Murray Butler*

A swift look at the American media's picture of teenagers shows them to be selfish, self-centered, and self-indulgent. In this picture, they crowd into malls to hang out and occasionally shop, spend idle hours watching television and movies, and are obsessed with drugs, sex, and self-destruction.

This picture is not the only true one. Teenagers today have a more active social conscience than in any previous generation. Their concern for others is obvious and easily tapped. Today's teenagers are surprisingly dependable and generous with both their time and their money.

A 1989 survey by the Independent Sector found that 58% of American teenagers volunteered their time to help others. Actually, more "selfish" teenagers gave of their time that year than adults, only 54% of whom volunteered. The widespread belief that teenagers are absorbed only by their own needs is simply not true.

Teenagers also gave generously. In 1989, half of all American teenagers contributed to charity. The average annual teenage gift that year was $46. This may not seem like much, but teenagers frequently have little spending money. The *total* dollar amount that year was close to one quarter of a billion dollars—a large drop in anyone's bucket.

Teenagers in 1989 averaged almost four hours of volunteer time *each week*, and more than one fourth of them gave five hours or more. They provided a total of 1.6 *billion* hours of volunteer time. The monetary value of their volunteer hours, when calculated by the minimum wage, is about $5.9 billion. Girls were more generous with their time than boys (65% of teenage girls volunteered, versus 51% of the boys), but we should remember that teenage boys are more often employed than girls.

Almost three quarters of teenage volunteerism is through organized programs and charities or in helping the elderly. It is not uncommon to see fourteen- and fifteen-year-olds helping feed the homeless at shelters and soup kitchens. Harvey Mandel of the St. Vincent de Paul–Joan Kroc Center in San Diego reports that about twenty teenagers volunteer there each week. Students from Point Loma High School served Thanksgiving dinner at the Center recently to more than a thousand street people.

Young people today are not passive observers of society's ills but active forces in shaping the national social conscience. Although teenagers sometimes feel ignored by the adult world, their concerns about peace, the environment, social equality for minorities, along with their compassion for the homeless make an important contribution to the political and moral dialogue of the nation.

Some other findings about teenagers' generosity:

- 90% of teenagers lent a hand when they were asked. This is hardly selfish resistance. But young people are usually shy and respond best when they are asked to help. Only one in four volunteered without being asked.
- 48% were recruited by friends, 26% by teachers or school officials, 20% by relatives. Family, friends, and school are evidently the forces that move young people to volunteer action.
- 73% of teenagers who regularly attend religious services volunteered, while only 34% of those who did not attend volunteered. Religion is apparently another powerful motivator for young people.
- Two thirds of students in schools that have volunteer programs said they gave time.

Teenagers say that the principal reasons for volunteering are a desire to be useful to others, enjoyment of the work, the need to do something good with their free time, and a desire to learn and get experience.

Many benefits come to teenagers when they volunteer. They become part of community-wide efforts. Since they put in as much effort as adults, they are treated as adults and experience the world as peers of adults. Their work earns them real gratitude and acceptance, which leads to greater self-esteem. They learn about the benefits of giving and sharing. They become part of the give and take of team effort. And most of all, they see that they have the power to make a difference in the world.

It is vital that young people be encouraged in their volunteer work. It helps them develop a social conscience and forms the next generation of leaders for society. Volunteering also helps them experience first-hand the physical, emotional, and spiritual benefits of philanthropic involvement.

There are some concrete things you can do to promote volunteer activity among teenagers:

- Find out what courses and programs involving community volunteer work are offered by the local schools.
- Work with local volunteer agencies and religious organizations to develop ways to tap the special talents and energy of young people.
- Write articles for local newspapers highlighting youth volunteerism. (You might be surprised to find yourself published.)
- Help the media publicize opportunities for young people to volunteer. Suggest to local radio, television, and cable stations that they feature teens working as volunteers, and help set up such stories.
- Work with local businesses to establish and publicize scholarships for teen volunteers.
- Prepare a weekly or monthly list of teen volunteer opportunities and distribute it wherever young people congregate—schools, youth clubs, scout organizations, churches and synagogues.

· And, most important, talk to your own teenagers about volunteering, follow their progress in what they choose to do, praise their work, and make it an important part of your family conversation. Your increased respect for your teenagers will pay untold benefits in your family life.

By helping support teenage volunteerism, you can have a powerful effect on your community and its young people. Through your efforts, hundreds of young people may pitch in to help others—and, by helping others, help themselves.

Not all teenagers go on to college. The habit of generous giving and volunteering is important in the lives of those who go to work or enter the armed forces after high school. These young people will become the backbone of the work force of America. Habits of generosity and volunteerism, instilled in young adulthood, will help next-generation families and communities grow and prosper, opening wide avenues of interest in their lives.

Sharing volunteer time with others helps break down class barriers and overcome prejudices, thus becoming a powerful force for uniting communities. It can also open up opportunities for personal and professional advancement that might have gone unnoticed, helping to bridge the growing gap between rich and poor.

Teenagers who go on to college will have countless opportunities for service and advocacy. Many colleges now offer degrees in the management of nonprofit institutions, thus validating the importance of philanthropy in modern society. There has been a significant increase in the number of graduates in social work—15% since 1954. Graduate schools at Yale, Indiana, and other institutions of higher education now have programs to study the nonprofit world in depth, encourage research, and publish scholarly reports about philanthropy.

Recently some 120 college presidents formed Campus Compact, which actively promotes public service in undergraduate education. College students are encouraged to volunteer for programs to tutor illiterate adults, build shelters for the homeless, mentor disadvantaged children, and engage in many other types of public service. According to one state governor, at least a million college students are needed for one program alone—tutoring children who are failing in school.

Campus Compact aims to make the service ethic an integral part of undergraduate life. It works with federal, state, and local governments to establish community service programs. It unites existing efforts, such as teaching adults to read and helping underprivileged children. And it promotes civic involvement on campus.

There are thousands of colleges in the United States and Canada, and the energy of students is boundless. Campus Compact is one way to channel those energies, as are student forums, rallies, political activism and commitment, environmental causes and work for social justice. The work of students for a better world is an essential part of the social compact of our free society.

In the spring of 1991 I am happy to report that according to *USA Today*, college students are going against the spring-break tradition of "beaches, bikinis, and beer" and volunteering their time to help those less fortunate than they. Students from the University of Pennsylvania went to Tijuana, Mexico, to build houses in an impoverished area devastated by rain, while forty-three students from Saint Michael's College in Vermont spent their spring break working with battered women in Washington, D.C. Students from Vanderbilt University went to Guatamala as tutors, while students from Boston College worked with the poor in Boston and Appalachia. What an inspiration to us all!

The Baby Boomers Approach Middle Age

Wealth is a means to an end, not the end itself. As a synonym for health and happiness, it has had a fair trial and failed dismally.

John Galsworthy

At the end of World War II, the birth rate increased dramatically and remained high for fifteen years. This generation, the "baby boomers," today ranges in age from 30 to 44. Now 66 million strong, they account for almost one third of the adult population of the nation.

The baby boomers are better educated and more prosperous than any previous generation, so how they handle their money has far-reaching consequences. According to a recent Independent Sector study, the baby boomers give generously to charity. Those aged thirty-five to forty-four were more likely to make a contribution than any other group. And the picture is getting brighter—86% of baby boomers made charitable gifts in 1989, up from 76% in 1987. Their average annual contribution was $956, less than that of people fifty-five to sixty-four ($1,420) and more than young adults eighteen to twenty-four ($484). The number of volunteer hours put in by baby boomers is also above the national average.

Perhaps the most significant fact about baby boomers is that their parents will, as they die, leave them astonishing amounts of money. Cornell University economist Robert Avery estimates that the baby boomers' parents have accumulated a collective net worth of more than $6.8 *trillion*. The largest intergenerational transfer of wealth in U.S. history is about to begin.

If the U.S. economy remains vibrant, the richest 1% of baby boomers will each inherit an average of $3.6 million, the next 9% an average of $400,000, and the rest an average of $50,000. The richest will become even richer. But a significant proportion of this money will go to a larger group—about 6 million people.

How will this money be used? Some economists predict that a large amount of this transferred wealth will go directly and quickly to philanthropy. Such a large transfer of wealth to nonprofit organizations may prompt the government to raise inheritance taxes. The federal estate tax now ranges from 37% to 55% of any estate exceeding $600,000 ($1.2 million if left by a couple). The tendency of state governments, on the other hand, has been to reduce or eliminate inheritance taxes.

How will you benefit if you are a baby boomer who will inherit? Most obviously, you will be more secure as you approach your senior years. You will also have a greater opportunity to review your personal, social, political, and spiritual values and to contribute significantly to the causes you believe in. Your gift of time and money can have a tremendous impact on the nation and the world at large. And you should begin now to plan what you want to do with your resources, so that when the time comes, you will be able to act and give effectively.

Most research indicates that wealthy Americans are very generous. The tradition of giving back to the community what it so abundantly gave to you is still strong. This is best done intentionally.

If you believe that your fortunes will increase significantly through inheritance, you need to review your priorities and interests. That way, your wealth and influence will have the effect they deserve. Ask yourself these questions:

· Have you considered that giving and community service can significantly improve your life?

- What are your most important values, and how might you have a significant and lasting effect on what is important to you?
- How can you take a more active and consistent role in the organizations you believe in?

Some baby boomers have already received their inheritance, and it's interesting to see how they have handled it. An article in the May, 1990 issue of *Fortune* magazine reported on several such heirs. When George Pillsbury inherited $1 million at age 40, he used his fortune to co-found Haymarket People's Fund, a Boston charity that supports groups other charities avoid, such as the El Salvador Sister City Project. Another baby boomer commented, "My grandmother gave to her hospital and zoo, but my generation was politicized through Vietnam, the women's movement, and the gay rights struggle."

Baby boomers have the opportunity to support and endow causes that their new political and social consciousness make appealing. New types of philanthropies are likely to be beneficiaries of major gifts. What are your values? You may have the opportunity to improve society in a major way by your gift. Causes like the environment, social justice and equality, human rights, peace, and help for the homeless may find new strength and effective impact through *your* gifts and talents.

Some mainstream charities may suffer from this shift in the patterns of giving. But human needs remain remarkably constant, and as each generation matures, its interests tend to become more conservative and protective. Many radicals of the counterculture have now mellowed. Jerry Rubin, a national symbol of civil disobedience in the 1960s, is now a stockbroker. United Way forecasters believe baby boomers will favor different causes than did their parents and thus change the distribution of funds to charity and volunteer efforts. But enduring values and the institutions that represent them will continue to attract strong support.

The Older the Better

What lies behind us and what lies before us are tiny matters compared to what lies within us.
Ralph Waldo Emerson

Older people, especially those between the ages of fifty-five and seventy-five, are more generous than any other age group. They are the backbone of charitable giving. There are some fifty-three million people in America fifty-five years old or older, more than 57,000 of them over a hundred years old.

People's choices as to where they give remain remarkably consistent. A recent article in the *New York Times* described two long-time donors to the *Times* Neediest Cases Fund, which began asking for support in 1912. Edith Lissauer, who died this year at 100 years of age, had given to the Fund every year since its inception. Hannah Hofheimer, 101, a New Yorker all her life, cannot remember when she didn't support the Neediest Cases Fund. This year she gave $1,000.

The typical American aged fifty-five to seventy-five donates approximately $1,200 each year to charity. This figure represents about 4% of annual income, and twice the national average, which is 2%. People older than seventy-five tend to give less, perhaps because their assets are smaller or their medical expenses greater. But they still give a 50% greater proportion of their income than do people twenty-five to thirty-four years old. According to the Roper Organization, those sixty years or older donated almost $6 billion to nonreligious charities, while those eighteen to twenty-nine gave only $2.8 billion.

Older people are also the standard bearers of volunteer activity. Despite their age and sometimes limited health, they are much more likely to volunteer than are younger people. Because they have more time to give, older people give more of their time as volunteers, if sometimes at a more leisurely pace. The elderly are also more positive and traditional in their attitudes about helping others. They recognize that religion and community have sustained them for decades and they feel it is important to repay what they have received.

People's values shift as they grow older. Friendships, family, community, health, peace of mind, and spiritual concerns become more important while making money, acquiring possessions, and succeeding in business enterprise diminish in appeal. This shift from outer-directedness to inner-directedness is a movement away from personal achievement and toward creativity. Philanthropic activity helps older people grow.

If stress and tension are the great enemies of the young and ambitious, then isolation, loneliness, and depression are the foes in later life. Many medical and behavioral experts regard volunteer activity as a primary means to guard against physical and emotional deterioration. "Stay active," they counsel.

We have all seen and marvelled at the energetic octogenarian, the spry ninety-year-old who shows up regularly for a volunteer assignment. There are many, like Dr. and Mrs. Norman Vincent Peale, who do not feel that reaching ninety is any reason to stop serving the community. They are both still active and dynamic, counseling and publishing their inspirational books and newsletters. The "graying of America," the rapid increase in the number of older people, can only have a beneficial effect on giving and volunteering.

Have you created a sizeable estate? Or have you accumulated a more modest amount but still care about how it is used? Now is the time to arrange how you plan to distribute your wealth. If you are over 50 and have any kind of assets you hope to pass on to your children, relatives, and charity, I urge you to talk to a tax accountant, estate lawyer, or financial planner.

You have worked hard to accumulate your estate—whatever its size—and I'm sure you have definite ideas about its disposition. Well, your federal and state governments also have ideas about how they would like to use your assets. If you miss a beat in estate planning, there is little doubt about the IRS's response. If you don't want a large piece of your estate used to bail out a poorly managed bank or pay for a $700 wrench for the Air Force, draw up an estate plan with expert advice—and implement it. Better to fund a shelter for the homeless than a congressional junket to the south of France.

If it hasn't happened already, someday soon your minister or charitable organization is going to ask you for a sizeable gift. And they should. It is their responsibility *to you* to ask. While you may be uncomfortable with thoughts of your own death, it *will* happen. It will do you no harm, and probably much good, to plan to give a portion of your estate to a cause or institution you believe in. Even if your assets are tied up in property, land, or a business and you cannot make an immediate gift, you can do some future planning. There are ways a gift can be made in the future so that it doesn't diminish your current income.

Almost everyone has *some* assets, even if it is only a life insurance policy, a modest home, and a car. Relatively few people die as paupers. Maybe now is the time to consider how you can channel some of what you have toward a gift after death. Planned gifts are probably the most common way that money is now given in the United States. There are a number of uncomplicated ways you can make a planned gift: charitable remainder trusts, gift annuities, lead trusts, and gifts of property with retained life interest, among others. Since tax laws, rules, and accounting principles change fairly often, you would be wise to speak to a financial planner or tax consultant as you explore these giving opportunities further.

Careful planning can ensure that most, perhaps all, of your estate funds end up going where you want them to go—rather than, automatically, to the tax till. And the people and values you cherish will be endowed, and their influence extended, far beyond your own lifetime.

THE GIVING PATH

The Giving Path

> There never was a person who did anything worth
> doing, who did not receive more than he gave.
>
> *Henry Ward Beecher*

In my seminars and lectures I like to review the natural course of a life of sharing, which I call "the Giving Path." The urge toward generosity to others usually starts early in life, then flows along a continuum with early family instruction at one end and a naturally sensitive and spontaneous benevolence at the other.

The Giving Path unfolds like this:

- *Beginnings*: Early parental teaching and examples help form childhood attitudes toward giving and money.
- *Reinforcement*: In early schooling teachers, parents, and religious instructors help form an "emotional set" about giving, sharing, philanthropy, and the value attached to money and possessions. Social responsibility is formed at this stage.
- *Actualization*: Children begin to actually experience giving and sharing themselves. These early experiences, sometimes wonderfully confusing and embarrassing, make lasting impressions on children. The extended family helps encourage and support children's generous impulses.
- *Independence*: Young people begin to help others, freely using their own resources as new but increasingly vested members of the community.

- *Intensification*: Teenagers and young adults commit themselves to causes requiring volunteer service, active identification, and giving.
- *Maturity*: Adults make a wholehearted investment in a cause, inspiring spiritual kinship. Large gifts and bequests are often the natural result of this devotion.

There is no single Giving Path. Everyone's life has twists and turns, lapses, defections, disenchantments, and resistances. Compassion and selflessness develop very early in life and largely determine adult behavior. Willingness, devotion, levels of participation and degrees of commitment are finely honed over a lifetime, but it is early experiences that exert the most powerful influence over everyone's adult patterns of volunteering and giving. Conviction, resiliency, and passion for a cause usually spring from early, sensitized encounters.

I have heard H. Ross Perot, who rose from very poor circumstances to become a billionaire, talk about his mother feeding the homeless during the Depression. No wonder Perot became a giver as an adult—he learned it at his mother's knee when he was young and poor. The same is true for me. My father and mother, who were lower-middle-class at best, were consistently generous. They gave regularly to their church, and when neighbors and strangers alike needed help—no matter who they were—my parents were ready to give. I probably learned everything I know about philanthropy before I ever left home. And chances are, most of you have too.

Religion and Giving

Do good with what thou hast, or it will do thee no good.

William Penn

Millions of people give money to causes they care about. The primary recipients of this great river of benevolence are religious institutions. Almost half of all giving goes to churches and synagogues and their schools, hospitals, hospices, recreation facilities, nursing homes, and relief efforts. Nearly $55 billion was given to religious institutions in 1989. Church giving easily eclipses every other kind of nonprofit activity.

Religious training is a powerful influence on giving and social responsibility. People who attend religious services are more active and committed to giving, sharing, and volunteering than people who do not. According to a Gallup Poll, the average regular churchgoer gives 2.4% of his income to philanthropic causes, while those who do not attend services give about 0.8%. The spiritual connection is the driving force behind much of the nation's benevolence.

All major religions teach compassion and community commitment, urging their members to love their neighbors and give to others. Religion instructs families and communities to forgive, be compassionate, and unite to meet social problems. As institutions they provide continuity in benevolence over the years. They teach by example and personal involvement, and they are trusted and respected. It is a rare religious institution that does not point its young people to a compassionate, caring, and responsible lifestyle.

Spiritual teachings influence many people to volunteer their time, talent, and treasure. Religious people give and share because they are taught that they are their brothers' keepers. It is no surprise, then, that about one half of all American adult churchgoers did volunteer work in 1989, as opposed to less than one third of nonworshipers.

For many of us, volunteering and giving represent what is right with the world. An act of sharing is an act of love.

In a world filled with hostility, suspicion, and greed, an act of giving is an expression of faith in the future. It is a spiritual display of fundamental goodness—goodness we learned through religious and parental instruction.

Churches and synagogues are places of worship and nurture. They offer paths to involve people in their communities in brotherhood and love. About 60% of Americans claim religious membership, and this membership accounts for an overwhelming majority of volunteer hours week in and week out. Religion is the mother of American philanthropy.

The Complex Motives for Giving and Sharing

> He who wishes to secure the good of others has already secured his own.
>
> *Confucius*

Why do you volunteer? What makes you give? Why do some causes pull powerfully at you while others have no appeal? Recent research has begun to uncover some of the complexities behind the decision to give.

There is seldom a single, shining motive underlying philanthropy. Rather, there are usually one or two dominant motives with a cluster of psychological influences supporting and energizing them. These influences are both conscious and unconscious, so that you may understand only part of your own reasons for giving or volunteering. And sometimes the hidden motives are more powerful than the ones we can easily identify.

Some motives are more publicly acceptable than others. Few people would admit they gave a large gift just to outdo a neighbor's donation, or that they sought social recognition by volunteering for the board of a charity. A donor will not likely tell you he made a large pledge to a charitable cause out of guilt for shady financial dealings. None of us is perfect. We all sugarcoat our motives. The important thing is to recognize the good and do it, regardless of our motives.

Your age, means, philosophy of life, upbringing, lifestyle, and education are all likely to underlie your motives for giving. One of the most generous people I have ever met is Richard Freeland, a very successful Pizza Hut franchisee in Fort Wayne, Indiana. This man earns millions of dollars every year and he gives away at least half of what he makes—the limit our tax laws allow. If you ask him why he is so generous, he will give you a modest reply. But I am convinced that Dick, a minister's son, was set on the Giving Path early in life.

Family influences, peer pressure, and social forces also influence the decision to support a cause. And of course, there are also more changeable factors. The ups and downs of the economy, the skill of a fund raiser, changes in tax legislation, even how a person feels on a given day all enter into decisions about giving.

We have a very incomplete understanding of the emotional triggers that prompt us to act. In the last analysis, an act of generosity is an act of love, and people have labored since the beginning of time to fathom the complexities of love. Greater understanding of human psychology makes it more and more possible to manipulate others. But for the most part we continue to make our decisions about giving—and about everything else—on the basis of parameters we have established deep inside our characters. To analyze your own motives, ask yourself the questions in these eight categories:

Opinions and attitudes

What do you believe about money and possessions, about giving and charity in general? How strong are your feelings about duty and obligation, and how high is your level of commitment to sharing? To what extent do you see giving as a way of protecting your specific lifestyle? What are your attitudes toward relatives, friends, and strangers in need? How do you feel about your current level of giving?

Personal Capabilities, Values and Needs

What is your level of need for recognition, admiration, and approval? How much do you need to demonstrate love and affection? What is your capacity for nurturing and caretaking? Your need for personal contact in volunteering? How much feedback do you need, how much "stroking?" How secure are you in your inner life and about other people? How much pleasure and personal meaning do you get from giving and volunteering? Do you need to feel connected, more closely bonded to others? How concerned are you about your own finances? How much control do you think you have over your own life and your goals?

Religious and Spiritual Influences

How involved are you in your own religion? How much time and money do you give? What is your understanding of social responsibility? Do you believe in the "Golden Rule?"

Individuals and Institutions

How involved are you in local community charities? How committed are you to national and international organizations? How much do you give, and how long have you been involved? How much do you care about those served by your cause? To what extent do you agree with the ideals and goals of the cause? How effective is the management of the organization? Does it accomplish its goals? Do you identify with its newer programs? How do you relate to the people who ask you for money?

Popularity of the Cause

What is the general opinion of the value of the cause you support? Has there been strong favorable or unfavorable publicity about it recently? Is the organization an elite one, or does it have a wide base? Do people give to it in order to be identified with its cause?

Appeals and Fund Raising Efforts

Were you convinced to give through strong personal persuasion by a fund raiser, or by a relative, friend, or someone you admire? Was there a powerful emotional appeal to give on television or other media? Did you give in order to put an end to persistent appeals? Did you decide to give after you volunteered some time? Did you give because the need was urgent, for famine relief or a medical emergency?

Social, Economic, and Political Forces

Did you choose your cause because of local or national economic conditions? Did you consider it because of a change in the law or tax rules, or because the government passed legislation favoring or opposing what the organization stands for? Did you choose your cause because of competitive or peer pressures? Did the cause come to your attention because of war or the threat of conflict?

Early Training

How were you influenced by early religious and spiritual training, by family example, by traditions or cultural indoctrination? Did you respond because of early traumatic or intense experiences?

As you can see, if you answered these questions honestly, your motives for choosing and supporting a cause are very complicated. At a given time, some motives will dominate others, and as you grow and change, so will your reasons for giving.

Beyond these motives for giving, conscious and unconscious, there are the benefits of giving. These are so strong and so positive that once you experience them, they themselves can become motives to adopt a life of sharing.

If you were to stop a few people on the street willing to tell you what troubles them most, I'll bet you would hear about health problems, stress, emotional confusion, low self-esteem, alienation, and lack of personal satisfaction. The benefits of philanthropy go right to the core of these human concerns. A philanthropic life provides relief from many of these contemporary ills, both for the receiver and the giver.

As research confirms the benefits of a life of sharing, and as doctors, clergy and therapists begin to recommend philanthropy for its healing powers, I believe that more and more people will choose the giving lifestyle. Though everything else in our society may grow more complex, these benefits can be trusted to bring order and well-being into our lives. And isn't that what we all want?

Praise, Recognition and Appreciation

> The deepest principle in human nature is the craving to be appreciated.
>
> *William James*

Most of us remember how good it felt to be praised when we were children. We liked the attention and we felt more valued as human beings. And naturally, we learned to do things that would earn us more praise and recognition.

There is a natural tendency to adopt behaviors that make us feel good. In their book *Life Is Uncertain, Eat Dessert First*, Sol Gordon and Harold Brecher divide this movement into three parts. First, we respond well to good feelings. Second, we try to experience good feelings again and again, being drawn to things that provide us consistent pleasure. Third, we become bored or dissatisfied with things that do not bring some kind of material or emotional reward.

Giving and sharing do not usually provide material rewards. Their benefits are psychological and physiological. Some of us can provide those rewards for ourselves out of a sense of self-satisfaction, but most of us turn to others for recognition. We want to know that others think we count and that our efforts make a difference. We even look for this recognition in the animal world. Pat a dog and watch its tail wag. Stroke a cat and listen to it purr.

And so it amazes me to see the neglect and indifference that greet many dedicated volunteers and donors. We are reared to look for rewards and we have a kind of special alertness when we do something good for others, like a child looking up to his parents after performing well. We saw our parents' special smiles of pleasure when they were praised for some kind deed or gift, and we want to smile that smile as well. It is the completion of a kind of unwritten contract: "I will give my time, talent and treasure, willingly and with no expectations . . . but it sure would be nice to get a little praise."

It passes my understanding why so many organizations give little or no thought to the art of praise and gratitude. They spend so much time and effort studying how to recruit volunteers and expand their fund-raising activities, then seem blind to the giver after the gift is given. Most nonprofit organizations have active and well-staffed developmental departments, but I have yet to see a reward and recognition department. If I were building an organization, I would hire the best "praise and appreciation" expert I could afford. It is critical to show gratitude continuously and systematically. Philanthropy is a people-to-people, emotionally based activity, and often there is a tremendous imbalance between the gifts and recognition of these gifts.

There are reasons why organizations may neglect the proper recognition of their donors and helpers. Nonprofit organizations are usually badly underfunded and run close to the edge of insolvency. The people in charge of running the organizations may be too busy and harried to consider thanking others. They may have lost their sympathy through overwork. They may feel that praise is not necessary, that virtue is its own reward. They may themselves be disappointed with how things are going. It may even be that the people in charge have never learned to thank others, but are self-absorbed, blind to the power of praise, or distrustful of others. If so, they should learn to praise others for their own sakes.

A little praise goes a long way in volunteering. Most volunteers and donors expect to give sacrificially and are aware of the depth of need that has called forth their commitment to the cause. They provide the labor, and the organization provides the structure and the mission. They don't expect lavish attention. They know their work itself will provide many satisfactions, not least from the people they help directly. And the camaraderie of co-workers is a wonderful lift along the way. But any organization is well advised to make a regular habit of giving praise and recognition. The people who give and volunteer are its life blood. They thrive on gratitude.

Many people who give freely and receive little thanks or praise may become disenchanted and drop away from the organization. They may shift their allegiance to a more appreciative cause. They may reduce their level of activity—fewer hours or a smaller donation. They may give up on philanthropy entirely. Or they may convince themselves that praise doesn't matter and discount the importance of their efforts, only to see their disappointment sneak back in the form of backbiting, criticism, or undermining others' work.

If you see people growing disenchanted with your organization because of lack of recognition, there are some steps you can take to avoid such unhappy results.

- Appoint yourself chairperson of the "praise and recognition" committee and make a list of all the people and efforts you think would respond best to appreciation.
- Look for other situations where a kind, encouraging word would boost morale.
- Discuss your list with the director of the organization, then put together a committee whose task it would be to organize recognition and praise.
- If you have the authority, bring your most dynamic people together and brainstorm ideas for appreciation.
- If you do a lot of fund raising, hold a special session to develop ways to thank your donors. Many organizations devote a lot of effort to attracting donors but none at all to thanking them, not even sending a computer-written letter of thanks. Failure to acknowledge donors is a sure-fire way to lose future support. A personal note, a certificate of appreciation, a phone call—all go far to build long-lasting relationships that turn one-time donors into committed friends.
- Take time in your own volunteer work to acknowledge others. In *The One Minute Manager* Ken Blanchard calls such activity "one minute praisings." These aren't contrived or artificial rituals, but specific acts of genuine appreciation. There is always something positive to praise in the work of others, even if it is hard to see at first. If we can lift the spirit and self-esteem of others, we can make a sour day sweet and a miserable day manageable. In his book *Love and Profit*, James Autry calls this the "art of caring leadership."
- Teach your children how valuable praise can be. Explain the positive role of appreciation to them. And praise them when they thank others.

Appreciation, acknowledgement, and praise cost absolutely nothing. But a kind word is valuable only when it moves from thought to speech. Words of praise do not diminish the speaker, and they build up the recipient. If you are looking for an effective way to use your personal power, praise the work of others. See what a difference you make.

S·E·V·E·N

PERSONAL POWER: ACTING ALONE AND TOGETHER

A Path To Greater Personal Power

There can be no greater argument to a man of his own power than to find himself able not only to accomplish his own desires, but also to assist other men in theirs; and this is that conception wherein consisteth charity.

Thomas Hobbes

How can we create change and make a difference for other people? Since we were children we have all heard about great saints and benefactors of humanity. Newspapers and television inform us about remarkable people who have done wonderful things for others. And we know that goodness, charity, and concern for our neighbors make life better for everyone.

There are, of course, remarkable people of exceptional intelligence, talent, or wealth who do great things. But the vast majority of present-day miracle workers are ordinary people of limited means. Some of these people are famous throughout the nation and world while others work quietly and consistently close to home to help their troubled neighbors. All of them change the world.

When I was a child someone told me that most people use only ten percent of their intelligence. As I grew, I wondered how I could use more of the other 90%. But as time passed, I decided I really didn't have any unusual ability to call upon powers special enough to make a difference in the world, and I more or less dismissed the idea. I think most of us have the same experience. We have heard of others who have achieved great things, but we see little indication of such powers in our own lives.

Yet many people accomplish so much. They develop successful careers or businesses, achieve financial security, build good marriages, and do a good job of raising and educating their children. But when they think of helping others they doubt whether they can make much of a difference.

This isn't hard to understand. For every book on the powers of giving and sharing, there are fifty on how to succeed in careers. For every college course on community responsibility, there are hundreds on technology and business. We simply haven't spent much energy teaching people how to get in touch with their personal powers to make a difference in the lives of others.

The source of our personal power is our beliefs. What we believe to be true and how we feel about ourselves determine what we think we can do. Our belief system is, to a large extent, a collection of convictions we have about ourselves. If we think we are too weak, too small, too powerless, to accomplish anything significant, we limit what we can experience in our lives. If you don't think you can do something, you probably can't.

You have doubtless had the experience of being told that something you wanted to do simply couldn't be done and then seeing someone else do it anyway. So many of our beliefs started out in fear and have held us back ever since. They limit the way we respond to challenges. For every person who, facing a difficulty, says "Let's work for a miracle," there are ten who will say "This is impossible." Our attitudes—our beliefs about what we think we can do—control what we accomplish. Some of us have walked away from great things in our lives because we were told we weren't capable enough and we believed it.

There's a deadly mental exchange, a one-two punch,

that knocks out our initiative and genius. Our belief system says, "This is impossible." Then our thought process says, "There's no need to even get involved. I think I'll go home."

Such a dialogue gives no consideration to the possibility of a miracle. We simply can't exercise our true abilities until we suspend denial of our ability long enough to rise to the occasion. We are often so weighed down by our negative beliefs about ourselves that our personal powers are smothered.

There are people who escape this negativity trap. An ordinary citizen champions a cause out of personal tragedy and forces Congress to change the law. A neighbor feels deeply about the plight of the stranded and founds the Travelers Aid Society. A mother loses a child and founds M.A.D.D. These people are often astonished at what they have created. At first they may have doubted they could have more than limited local impact. But they were willing—willing to get involved, to make noise, to investigate, to consider the possibilities. Once they moved beyond their own fears, vistas opened up ahead of them. Circumstances changed because they were asking questions, talking to others, looking for advice and support, and planning to change the status quo.

People like these tell me that there comes a point when they begin to believe they can create something new. A dream starts to grow, a conviction that they have powers to draw on. There's a shift from "what if" to "maybe, if God helps." A kind of spiritual intervention seems to occur that gives them faith in their abilities. Dr. Robert Schuller calls it "possibility thinking." These people see themselves in partnership with a spiritual being, then persevere because they believe they and their work are blessed and empowered.

For others the road is less mystical. By making a beginning and letting the situation unfold, their faith in their

abilities is confirmed, and they are more and more willing
to take risks. M. Scott Peck says of this stage: "Benevolence is community. There can be no community without involvement and no involvement without vulnerability and no vulnerability without risk."

In order to expand our personal powers, we need to
suspend what we believe about our limits. We need to set
aside negative thoughts about a situation and our ability
to change it. We can't help having these thoughts, but
that doesn't mean we have to act on them. We need to
become involved and investigate, heedless of discourag-
ing, cautionary words—in our own minds or from others.
We need to increase our belief in our own potential. We
need to have faith in spiritual guidance and support. And
finally, we need to be willing to persevere, to be vulnerable, to risk failure.

More than one person who was discouraged in the
seeming failure of a business career has told me that
when he began to move away from self-interest and toward concern for others, his life, career, and business
changed dramatically. His narrow focus on himself had
locked up personal power that could only be unleashed
when his horizons widened.

Many people yearn to commit themselves to a cause, to
give themselves wholly to something worthwhile. Few
people accomplish this completely. But in addition to
saints, there are millions of ordinary people who have
made important contributions simply through dedicated
service. You don't need great expertise or sacrifice to
produce results. You do need devotion, commitment,
willingness, and faith.

When you begin to use your personal power to help
others, people benefit from your work. You feel a sense of
accomplishment, and your belief in your ability grows.
You enjoy things more and have a greater sense of control
over your life, which leads to greater self-acceptance and a

sense of self-worth. Your physical, emotional, and mental well-being increase. And your vital power becomes an example to others.

The faithful exertion of effort produces all these benefits. While we can certainly use our power for selfish goals, the full range of benefits comes to us only in the accomplishment of good for others. Acts of selfishness may be appealing in the short run but carry within them the seeds of dissatisfaction.

When you begin to use your personal powers for giving and sharing, you should consider these ways to make your experience more successful:

- Examine why you have chosen this particular cause and whether it fits your talents.
- Be innovative. Think differently about what you can contribute.
- Be bold, take risks, and think big.
- Talk about your project with everyone. Tell them what you need. You never know where resources—even miracles—will come from.
- Ask help from friends, relatives, every friendly—and even not so friendly—source.
- Put principles and goals before personalities. The world is far from perfect, and people will often disappoint you. Accept others for what they are and move ahead. Be willing to lead.
- Don't drown yourself in your task. Keep your balance. You have a dream: give it your best effort, but also take time to laugh and enjoy life along the way. Smell the flowers. You can reduce stress and attract others with your joy. Turning your goal into a combat mission does not produce harmony and well-being.
- Start out in low gear. Take your time, move with caution and concern for others. Breakneck speed and im-

mediate results are rarely needed. Pace yourself and avoid disillusionment and burnout.

· When you meet an insurmountable obstacle, just sit with it for a while. Get advice from experts. Give your frustration and impatience time to diminish. This may not be easy, but it will save you time, energy, and emotional stress in the long run. Faith and prayer are good partners at such times.

Your attitudes influence the outcome of your efforts at giving. Try to avoid dreams of personal glory. We all act from mixed motives, but we can all work to keep them as pure as possible. There's nothing wrong with wanting recognition and praise, but things often go awry when the desire for personal fame, control, or privilege becomes the primary motive for giving.

Often people enter into charitable work without joy or positive feelings. Some of us were brought up to believe that sacrifice, drudgery, duty, and obligation are the hallmarks of effective sharing, believing that if it doesn't hurt, we're not doing it right. These people don't experience the joy and satisfaction inherent in their work—or, at best, are indifferent to it.

Acts of generosity should nourish the people who do them. If you aren't getting much satisfaction from your work of giving, maybe you should look for a cause that would be closer to your heart. There's already enough drudgery and sacrifice in the world, but hardly enough joy.

If you're a person who just can't seem to get much good feeling out of any activity, maybe you should challenge your ideas about what you're allowed to be in your life. With some courage and willingness, you can have the power to transform your life. The joys in the life of giving and sharing are very real, and you deserve your share of them. As Drs. Robert Ornstein and David Sobel point out in their book *Healthy Pleasures,* altruism is healthy: "The great surprise of human evolution may be that the highest form of selfishness is selflessness."

And what about other people? When you begin to work in a volunteer organization, you're likely to find that people fit into three categories: those who cooperate and support you; those who are indifferent, remote, or unavailable; and those who seem to work at cross-purposes. Also, volunteers are all too human. After a very short time you will come up against the reality that people are on occasion rude, crude, and indifferent—and who are *you* not to have your feelings hurt? Sometimes frustration and conflict, lack of sensitivity, indifference, and ingratitude will combine to put you on edge. Working with others requires tolerance and patience, particularly when everyone is volunteering their time.

But try a smile, a quiet assurance, a word of praise, and watch how they can defuse conflict. Try not to take yourself too seriously. If you do these things and keep a sense of perspective, I promise you that your own personal effectiveness will increase and your cause will prosper.

Some People Who Used Their Personal Powers

The thing which counts is the striving of the human soul to achieve spiritually the best that it is capable of and to care unselfishly not only for personal good, but for the good of all those who toil with them upon the earth.

Eleanor Roosevelt

A Tragedy that Produced A New Law

In September of 1989, Howard and Connie Clery waved goodbye to their lovely nineteen-year-old daughter as she left home for college. Not long after, they received a call telling them she had been brutally raped and murdered in her dormitory room. They were devastated—and enraged, when they found that the ineffectual and closed-mouth campus security people had known the killer had been known to be a campus troublemaker. Out of their grief came a plan: with no formal knowledge of what might be involved, the Clerys put their agony into action. They lobbied Congress for a federal law making it mandatory that colleges report the numbers and types of crimes committed on campus.

After concerted effort on the part of the Clerys, Congress passed and President Bush signed the Student Right to Know and Campus Security Act of 1990. If colleges fail to provide accurate crime statistics, they risk the loss of federal funds. Now prospective students and their parents can discover the true state of campus security. As Mr. Clery has said, "Hopefully this will help to reduce the scourge of violence on our college campuses—much of which is committed by students because of drug and alcohol abuse."

Here is a couple who were moved to action by their tragedy. They used their energies to get Congress to pass a law that will lessen the likelihood of other parents' experiencing losses like theirs. They saw the national implications in their personal loss and had the courage, determination, and willingness to take the steps necessary to change the status quo. Many lives may be saved as a result.

Answered Prayers and Then Some

According to a *New York Times* story in December of 1990, Cheryl Woods, a Kansas City nurse, lost her paycheck just before Christmas. The $400 check was already endorsed and could have been cashed by whoever found it. It was found by Rosemary Pritchett, a homeless mother of three young children, who had just put in a bid on an abandoned house with the little money she had left. Mrs. Pritchett said it never crossed her mind to cash the check. She looked up Mrs. Woods' phone number from the address printed on the check and used her last quarter to make the call.

When Mrs. Woods came to pick up the check, she found the Pritchetts in a homeless shelter and offered a $25 reward. Mrs. Pritchett declined. "Just give me a note of thanks I can show my children. I want them to know that when you find something, somebody has lost it." Only when Mrs. Woods threatened to leave the $25 on the floor and walk away did Mrs. Pritchett accept the reward.

The next day Mrs. Pritchett's bid on the abandoned house was accepted and she moved her children and few possessions into a house that was little more than a shell. The walls were crumbling, and vandals had ripped out the wires and plumbing. A few days later, Mrs. Woods visited and found the Pritchetts trying to repair the house with only a hammer and screwdriver. She decided to do something about the situation.

The first thing she did was to ignore her husband's warning that the job would break her heart. She took up the Yellow Pages, worked her way through the contractor section, and finally found a contractor who agreed to become supervisor without charge. Another contractor offered to install a free water heater, and a supplier built windows and donated fixtures. Mrs. Woods's retired uncle also worked on the restoration.

When newspapers and television picked up the story, the project began to take on a life of its own. Contractors and builders offered free labor and equipment. Debris was removed free and total strangers came forward to help. In the end, $30,000 worth of labor and equipment was donated. It all happened because one person cared enough to help a neighbor who had helped her. And everyone benefited.

The Magic of Youth

Brian O'Connell in his book *Volunteers in Action* tells how young Trevor Ferrell was watching television on a cold December night in 1983. The news showed Philadelphia street people huddled over steam vents to stay warm. Trevor pleaded with his father to take him downtown so that he could deliver a blanket and pillow.

This single visit became a nightly mission of mercy. As word of Trevor's generosity spread, contributions from all over the country poured in to what became known as Trevor's Campaign. Some 250 volunteers now cook and deliver soup and sandwiches nightly to the homeless. A 33-bedroom rooming house, anonymously donated, is being renovated as a day shelter for 100 homeless people. Trevor, now twelve years old, focussed attention on the needs of homeless people and showed the nation the difference one young person can make.

At Home At Last

For many years Robert Hayes, thirty-two, has visited homeless shelters and appeared in court to prod New York City into providing places for homeless people to sleep. This advocate for the homeless sued the city in 1979 and obtained a consent decree to provide clean, safe shelter to every homeless person who seeks it. In 1982 he founded the Coalition for the Homeless, which has grown into three national organizations. The Coalition's activities include running a camp for homeless children and feeding thousands of people every day.

Giving and Caring Keep Us Going

In 1988, Arnolta Williams received the President's Volunteer Action Award. At ninety-one, she had devoted seventy years to helping the poor and uneducated youth of Jacksonville, Florida. She was a founder of the Jacksonville Urban League and the founder of the Gateway Nursery, which serves low-income working mothers. She has volunteered for the Red Cross, the Council on Aging, the YWCA, and has been chairperson on the Foster Grandparents Program, a board member of Florida Community College, a member of the Mayor's Commission on the Status of Women, and a delegate to the 1981 White House Council on Aging. She has spent her life helping the young, the old, the poor, and the uneducated. Her energy and personal powers have made her a remarkable woman.

Dreams That Fly

Dale Shields, a Floridian who moved from Michigan in 1975, has saved more than 16,000 pelicans and other birds hurt or disabled by boats, fishhooks, pesticides, automobiles and other man-made hazards. At first, his efforts were random and limited. He loved the beauty of the pelican and he wanted to do more, but he didn't have the time and resources. When he realized he couldn't help all the birds by himself, he began to ask around and decided to risk starting a nonprofit organization—the Pelican

Man's Bird Sanctuary, a bird and wildlife refuge. From a part-time one-man effort, his dream has become a 4,000-member organization with 150 volunteers who rescue and care for birds at the sanctuary. In 1990 President Bush cited him as one of the "Points of Light." Dale says he appreciated the citation but was even more pleased by a letter from a twelve-year old who told him that she was so inspired by his work that she plans to become a veterinarian.

Lumpy Willie

When William was five years old, his seemingly normal body began to change. Lumps developed on his forehead and neck, soon spreading to his hands and back. Diagnosed as Von Recklinghausen's disease (a form of neurofibromatosis), the odd-shaped fibroid tumors soon completely covered his body. He quickly picked up the nickname "Lumpy Willie."

To compound his misery, he parents both died when he was twelve, leaving him alone with his physical nightmare.

As a teenager, he met with cruel rejection. No girl would go out with him. Restaurant waitresses hated to serve him. He refused to look at himself in a mirror. Life got worse and worse for Lumpy Willie, "The Ugliest Man in Canada."

To numb his misery, he turned first to alcohol and then to other drugs. His anger and desperation led him into crime. By the time he was twenty-one, he had been arrested more than fifty times for petty theft and finally for armed robbery. At twenty-five, he was sent to prison for life. Rejected by his fellow inmates, he spent much of his prison time in solitary confinement.

A resident in neurosurgery, Darrell Davis, heard of his predicament. Eager to experiment with a new surgical procedure that held out some hope for victims like Willie, Dr. Davis asked for an interview with him. He was flatly denied. Willie's bitterness had closed all doors of hope for him.

But over a period of months, Dr. Davis's persistence paid off. Willie met with him and, after several conversations, consented to a limited surgical experiment on his face. Over the next twelve months, Dr. Davis performed sixteen operations in more than thirty hours of surgery. He worked obsessively, at no charge, to liberate Willie from his personal prison.

On Willie's birthday in July of 1963, Dr. Davis came to his cell with a brightly wrapped gift. When the paper was torn away Willie found himself looking in a mirror and unable to believe what he saw: a normal man with a normal face. He cried. He laughed. He hugged his benefactor. Willie wasn't lumpy any more!

The change in his life was immediate. He became a model prisoner. Within six months, he and Dr. Davis stood before a judge and heard him declare Willie a free man, returning him to society to begin a new life. From then until his death four and a half years later of internal complications from the disease, the man once known as "The Ugliest Man in Canada" was one of its outstanding citizens.

Dr. Davis's gift of skill, work, and hope not only brought new life to a condemned man, it also initiated an unending wellspring of joy in the young doctor's life.

Daily Use of Personal Powers

As part of the White House's Points of Light Initiative to encourage volunteerism, President Bush honors individuals, nonprofit groups, and companies that are "making a difference in their communities." The White House estimates that by recognizing one person or organization each day, it will have named 1,000 Points of Light by Inauguration Day in January of 1993. Some of the people and groups recently cited by the White House are:

Justin Lebo, Saddle Brook, New Jersey, a thirteen-year-old who rebuilds old bicycles for needy children. He runs a lemonade stand, saves his allowance, and collects donations to raise money to purchase bike parts.

Florence Ziedman, Buffalo Grove, Illinois, who began volunteering for the Hines Veterans Administration hospital in Hines, Ill., during World War II and still visits patients at the hospital today.

Volunteers of Lakeview Shepherd Center, New Orleans, Louisiana, who offer assistance to senior citizens such as rides to doctors' appointments and food delivery.

Minerva Soerheide, Mount Hermon, California, who devotes at least forty hours each week to tutoring adults in English, including workplace literacy, reading, and writing. Ms. Soerheide also tutors Hispanics trying to obtain U.S. citizenship.

Mitchell Cardell Baldwin, Birmingham, Alabama, who, after growing up in a housing project, founded CHAMP (Caring Helps Another Make Progress), which provides positive role models and weekly activities for young people in a neighborhood housing project.

Connie Harris, Springfield, Oregon, who, drawing on her own experience as a teenage parent, volunteers as leader of the Birth to Three support group, which encourages young mothers to continue their education and helps them become better parents.

Davarian Baldwin, Beloit, Wisconsin, a teenager who for three years has been a member of the Beloit Positive Youth Development program, which helps young people in low-income neighborhoods appreciate their community and the environment. He founded a rap group that offers advice to young people, is the president of the Urban 4-H program, and each summer leads a camping trip for city youths.

Gudrun Gaskill, Golden, Colorado, who in 1972 began to help build the Colorado Trail, a string of hiking paths and campsites that spans 470 miles. Today, Ms. Gaskill, sixty-three, coordinates the volunteer work crews, handles all paperwork, and still helps with the physical labor of improving the trail.

Harvest House, Lansing, Michigan, whose volunteers search the streets for the homeless and inform them about Harvest House programs, such as hot-meal services and substance-abuse education.

Ron Dickey, El Paso, Texas, a quadriplegic who volunteers twenty hours a week for DARE (Disabled Ability Resource Environment), offering disabled people advice and friendship.

David Goldstein, Albany, New York, who volunteers nights for the Samaritans, a suicide-prevention program, and helps recruit additional volunteers.

John L. Oliver, Midland, Texas, a retired engineer who drives seventy miles every Friday to the West Texas Children's Home to tutor children in mathematics.

Volunteers of Rosemont Center, Columbus, Ohio, who provide counseling and job-skills training, as well as assistance with support groups and field trips, to the adolescent girls at this residential and day-care facility.

Volunteers of Community Service Project, Rockland, Maine, where 100 young people help the elderly and disabled with home repairs and maintenance.

Clare Allen, Nashville, Tennessee, a volunteer for the Harris-Hillman School who tutors disabled children daily and helps them with physical therapy and other living skills.

William Smith, Donora, Pennsylvania, a seventy-seven-year-old who helps his neighbor, a divorced mother of two children living on a fixed income, by providing transportation and buying the family food, clothing, and school supplies.

These are just a few of the many people who use their personal powers to make the world better for others. They are the people we are talking about in this book—people who have sought and found a meaningful life through sharing. Don't you want to be one of them?

Self-Help and Support Groups

Through the community of AA and similar fellowships modeled on it, millions upon millions have received healing, millions upon millions have found meaning in their lives. No other phenomenon has had such an impact for good in a nation.

M. Scott Peck

We are a troubled society, beset by internal and external pressures. One of the best remedies we have discovered for our troubles is the support group. Millions of people have found peer support groups to be an amazingly successful path to recovery, whether from alcoholism, cancer, or divorce. The National Self-Help Clearinghouse in New York City estimates that there are at least 500,000 self-help groups serving 15 million members.

The proliferation of support groups is a uniquely American reaction to personal crisis. People in trouble can turn to others with similar difficulties. The support-group phenomenon is pure philanthropy—suffering people welcoming each other and offering their love, compassion, and assistance.

Several features are basic to all self-help groups. First, participation is limited to people who have experienced the kind of suffering the group exists to alleviate. There are no salaried leaders who make wise pronouncements based on professional knowledge. There are no lectures, only people sharing their experience with other people. There is no hierarchy, only a very rudimentary organization in which everyone enjoys equal status.

Second, the responsibility for change and recovery rests squarely on the individual member. The groups provide a supportive environment where change and growth can take place, but each member is the architect of his own recovery. The self-help movement stresses tangible results. It rests on a very American assumption: bring together the resources, take responsibility for the problem, and solve it.

Every available statistic shows that support groups help people make real and lasting change. Most groups are made up of people in similar circumstances coming together to share experience, information, and emotional support. And those who merely listen often get as much out of the experience as those who actively participate.

The self-help movement began in 1935 with the founding of Alcoholics Anonymous. In 1950, AA was followed by Al-Anon, a self-help group for spouses, and children, and parents of alcoholics. In recent years, awareness of the many problems that can best be solved through concerned support has caused the number of self-help groups to skyrocket. There are now groups focussing on divorce, drug and dependency problems, isolation and loneliness among single and elderly people, mental illness, life-threatening diseases, and compulsions ranging from gambling and overeating to shoplifting, sex, and workaholism. Victims of diseases, rape, incest, and drunk driving have come together, as have abusive parents, parents of runaway children, and recently released felons. People in various kinds of minorities band together for mutual support. Although by definition the membership in an anonymous group cannot be accurately tallied, estimates place the membership in AA at two million, with Adult Children of Alcoholics (ACOA) and Al-Anon not far behind.

There are four basic kinds of support groups:

- *Addictions* such as alcohol, drugs, food, gambling, and work.
- *Illnesses* both physical and mental, from cancer and heart disease to schizophrenia and phobias.
- *Personal crises* from divorce, widowhood, and the death of a child, to physical abuse and incest.
- *Relatives and friends* of people with serious problems, such as Al-Anon, ACOA, Al-Ateen, and the parents of suicidal children.

There is a positive relationship between self-help groups and more general kinds of volunteering and charitable giving. A ten-year study at Stanford University showed that terminally ill cancer patients who participated in weekly support groups survived for a period nearly twice as long as those who did not. Consistent participation in self-help groups will teach a member to care for other people. As with philanthropic activity, people heal themselves while helping to heal others. And for millions of people, self-help groups dispel loneliness and isolation and help focus concern on other people.

The sagging economy has recently led to large cutbacks in government spending for social services. Support groups cannot meet all these needs, but they help focus the intelligence and compassion of individual people on real problems, and frequently lead to solutions. Given the realities of our economy, they may be the backbone of social progress for years to come. People who successfully manage their problems and who are aware of similar problems in others are much more likely to volunteer, give to a cause, and work for its success. Another study indicates that as many as 40% of all people in the "helping professions" came from troubled families and have fought through their own problems, often with the help of self-help and support groups.

How do you join this effort? Examine your life. Perhaps you are already *aware* of a problematic area. Look around, ask about groups dealing with your situation. If you can't find one, start one. All you need is a room to meet in, a little publicity, an hour or so to spare on a regular basis, and enough love and concern to share yourself with others in similar need. You can change the world while you change your own life.

E · I · G · H · T

EMERGENCE OF GLOBAL PROBLEMS

The Global Need for Giving

Help thy brother's boat across, and lo!
thine own has reached the shore.
Hindu proverb

Older generations tend to view philanthropy as traditional charity, giving to the disadvantaged to eliminate
suffering. Younger people are more apt to see it as a
complex system, with government bearing the chief responsibility and private initiative providing special assistance. Clearly, neither the state nor private initiative can
eliminate or even alleviate poverty, suffering, and social
injustice singlehandedly. The job requires a progressive,
sensitive society in which personal commitment helps
provide the resources for many basic needs. Philanthropy,
working through its many different channels, can demonstrate ways to resolve social ills.

Perhaps a quarter of the planet's population has a
woefully inadequate standard of living. Adequate food
and shelter, clothing, medical care, and literacy are beyond the reach of millions. They live in grinding, searing
poverty, and simple survival dominates their lives.

All countries, even the most advanced, have citizens
who suffer poverty, illiteracy, discrimination, and disenfranchisement. But the severity of conditions and the

ability of both government and private citizens to respond to these needs varies greatly from country to country.

For the sake of contrast, consider Cleveland, Ohio, and a typical village in Ethiopia. Cleveland, which has an illiteracy rate of 7% or 8%, also has millions of well-educated residents and thousands of teachers, schoolrooms that are empty at night, community centers, funds for books and paper—the capability, should enough citizens exert themselves, to end illiteracy almost overnight.

But a typical village in the highlands of Ethiopia may have an illiteracy rate of 70%. The country is torn by civil war, drought, famine, oppressive government control, poverty, high infant mortality, and a crumbling ecosystem. There is no government support for books, paper, pencils, or schoolrooms. Some of the population is literate but only at a rudimentary level. Certainly few citizens are able to instruct. The government uses most of its money for the military, which leaves very little to train and deploy teachers. The only substantial philanthropic structure is based on governmental foreign aid and assistance from such groups as OXFAM, CARE, UNICEF, Christian Aid, World Vision, and Save the Children. But neither governments nor groups such as these can resolve the problem of illiteracy.

Large populations in many countries all over the world suffer chronic poverty. The governments of most of these countries are virtually powerless. They lack the resources and sometimes the commitment to raise their own people's standard of living. Private philanthropy in these countries is limited, personal, and often misunderstood.

Public benevolence in all countries is shaped by local and regional cultural values and religious customs. In North America the roots of civic virtue are in religion. Citizens demonstrate their benevolence by giving of their money, talent and time. In some Asian cultures, charity is based on the family and is largely extended to relatives and the community, loans and guidance for local businesses or family members in need. Very few people think in terms of national or global responsibility.

Yet people in all cultures have an urge to help others in distress. This tendency can be fostered—as it is in many advanced societies—or blunted, in societies where the struggle to satisfy even the most primitive needs occupies all of human existence. But virtually all people experience a conscious or unconscious struggle between self-interest and compassion for others, between acquisition and generosity.

In economically limited societies, people who share give time and effort rather than money. The generous cooperation of people in third world countries often astonishes visitors from developed nations. Sri Lanka, off the south coast of India, is a rural, agricultural nation with a per capita income of perhaps $350. Yet philanthropy is very much a part of this indigenous culture. People regularly give their *time* to public projects or to assist their neighbors. A good deal of aid comes from worldwide organizations, but the programs are staffed and run by thousands of local volunteers. The people think in terms of national needs.

Some African nations, on the other hand, are deeply divided by tribal and regional loyalties that restrict their sense of responsibility for others. The primary unit of loyalty is the tribal group; all resources are acquired for your tribe, and the suffering of a neighboring tribe is none of your concern. While there is a high level of sharing within the tribe, there is little cooperative spirit between tribes. Not surprisingly, competition—even war—is often the normal state of affairs.

Christianity and Islam as well as supra-tribal governmental action can broaden these tribal loyalties to include others. But sometimes even these forces are harnessed in support of tribal competition. In the future, as tribal communities move to embrace each other, the possibilities will increase for social change through philanthropy. This reality may now seem a long way off in Africa, but the knowledge that it *is* possible is incentive enough to bring the joy of giving to the lives of many Africans.

There is no possibility that governments can meet all the enormous needs of poorer nations. Philanthropic action is the mainstay for much, if not most, improvement in the lives of people in many parts of the world. The necessity for giving and sharing on the world level has never been higher than it is now.

I can see three classes of nations, divided according to natural resources, industrial capacity, and standard of living. Each has different levels and forms of civic idealism and philanthropic urgency.

Industrially Advanced Nations

Western Europe, North America, Japan, Korea, Israel, Australia and New Zealand, Saudi Arabia, and some Latin American nations are technologically advanced. Most of them have a high standard of living and an effective central government with some form of capitalist economy. They have a strong sense of community responsibility and, in some of them, philanthropy flourishes. They also give to help other developing nations. And to some extent, their philanthropic approach is global.

Industrially Developing Nations

Most of Latin America, Eastern Europe, North Africa, China, Turkey, South Africa, and some countries in

Southeast Asia have emerging economies, substantial resources, and a decent if modest standard of living for most of their people. But they also have substantial poverty and disenfranchisement, large rural and agrarian populations, partial literacy at best, and rudimentary social services. For most of these nations, philanthropy is internal and less generous, primarily because of their lower standard of living. Most human service activities are carried out by volunteers on a local level only. Governments vary in strength and effectiveness, and political upheaval sometimes hampers social progress. Many of these countries depend on outside aid. They are limited in what they can export to help others and often have enormous debt to more advanced nations.

Underdeveloped Nations

Ethiopia, Sudan, Kampuchea, Vietnam, Lebanon, Central Africa, much of India, Pakistan, Afghanistan, and Burma are some of the most disadvantaged nations. They are chronically beset by war, famine, drought, political upheaval, primitive economies, plundered ecosystems, limited natural resources, widespread illiteracy, unmanageable government debt, runaway population growth, and tragically inadequate health care. These nations have only the most basic and direct public benevolence—people helping each other to survive.

Charitable organizations from many advanced countries supply basic human needs, yet demand for goods and services far outstrips the supply. Money and resources are scarce, but human compassion is plentiful. Mother Teresa's India missions for the poor are one example of the kind of local service possible with help from international giving. In most of these countries, civic service focuses on community and individual family needs. Their societies, disrupted by war, famine, and over-population, lack the resources to raise the standard of living substantially. Some, in fact, experience a continuous decline in living standards.

The world press provides jarringly realistic accounts of the stresses faced by individuals, families, and communities in the underdeveloped nations. Advanced nations are thus made more and more aware of the complex and chronic nature of these problems. Relief and development organizations provide aid, but the demand for assistance far exceeds the available contributions of money, resources, and technology.

Some underdeveloped nations have promising resources that could, over time, help them become self-sufficient. Other countries are too overpopulated, resource-poor, or economically paralyzed to be able to achieve self-sufficiency on their own. One of the challenges for aid and development organizations is the problem of how best to allocate funds and resources, particularly when available resources can meet only limited immediate needs. Survival has to be weighed against self-sufficiency efforts. The problem is further compounded by weak and poor governments that plunder or mismanage foreign aid to ensure continued political control. Emerging economies, supported by huge philanthropic outlays, are sometimes devastated by political self-interest and the corruption of their leaders.

All nations—not just the poorer ones—have poverty and illiteracy, abuse of human rights, environmental pollution, and ecosystem destruction. To resolve these problems both government and concerned citizens need to band together. Where governments falter, private initiative, local charities, and national advocacy must step in and shoulder the burden.

Most contributions by individuals are earmarked for domestic use. It seems most people follow the rule of "charity begins at home," with "home" being defined as within a forty-mile radius. Donations to the United Way and the collections of church organizations are almost always dispersed locally. Data from a recent survey suggests that donations by Americans to international relief may not exceed $200 million—a small sum compared to U.S. foreign aid. Religious donations may exceed this amount, but it is difficult to know the extent to which religious funds find their way overseas as development aid and relief.

In disadvantaged countries and in the poverty-stricken regions of developing nations, calamity and chaos are more enduring than international philanthropy, disease and despair more prevalent than health and hope. As global economic and ecological systems deteriorate, the plight of underdeveloped countries will worsen. Human need will escalate.

The developing nations will also suffer for many years to come from the burden of borrowing to become self-sufficient and to advance technologically. As taxes increase and rural unemployment grows, some of the resources for community human services will shrink. This will interrupt many service programs, slow the movement toward self-sufficiency, and increase the ranks of the poor. Few countries have the oil of Venezuela, Nigeria, or Indonesia, or precious-metal reserves like those in South Africa. Most nations put their investment into agriculture. These economies are subject to the fluctuating prices on the international market and the vagaries of the weather. Debt reduction, political unrest, ravaged ecosystems, and shifts in demand for agricultural products will limit the development of many countries for the foreseeable future.

Charitable giving is an important part of public and private life in most of Europe, North America, and some Asian countries. But the charity of the rich nations cannot cope with the poverty and other needs of developing countries. And as their own problems grow, advanced nations will doubtless become more ambivalent about a larger global commitment and revert to more insulated charity that benefits their own community. Yet all nations need to be concerned about their suffering neighbors. We cannot, in the twenty-first century, walk away from our ever-expanding responsibilities. We need to become globally philanthropic, both as individuals and as nations.

Government, Economics, and Cultural Values

> Each of us will one day be judged by our standard of life—not by our standard of living; by our measure of giving—not by our measure of wealth; by our simple goodness—not by our seeming greatness.
>
> *William Arthur Ward*

Benevolence is heavily influenced by government policy, the state of the economy, and cultural values. Government can assume the role of enlightened enabler and provider or it can seriously discourage private initiative. A downturn in the economy can dry up funds available for giving. And a community's cultural values shape the nature and content of giving and volunteerism. Limited vision and exclusionary practices can deeply restrict both aid to underdeveloped countries and domestic service. Let's look more closely at how some of these factors affect a nation's philanthropic behavior.

Government Influence

Governments are often inconsistent, greedy, and oppressive. At times they reflect the will of the people who gave them power; at other times, they march to their own tune. But in almost all nations, the government is the largest contributor to the national welfare. In order to serve, support, and rule, governments levy taxes that can range from fair and equitable to suffocating. Taxes can favor business enterprise but penalize workers, make it easy to accumulate wealth or be so restrictive that the acquisition of any wealth is impossible. Tax policies can favor redistribution of wealth to serve the population or enhance the fortunes of the mega-rich.

In Japan, tax policy makes it difficult for powerful businessmen to accumulate great personal wealth. In some oil-rich Middle East nations, a handful of leaders may own the majority of the nation's assets and have personal fortunes in the billions. And while it's true that much of this accumulated wealth is returned to the people in benevolent gestures and support for services, there are those who would question the right of anyone to amass great wealth that does not circulate for the good of all. A serious imbalance in wealth often produces a two-class state—the super-rich and the multitudinous poor.

A benevolent and responsive government, on the other hand, can do a great deal to foster philanthropy and voluntarism. The task is more difficult when much of the population is impoverished, the government is financially overextended by borrowing from other nations, and the super-rich—like the late President Marcos of the Philippines—are driven by greed.

There are many ways for government policy to encourage the overall climate for philanthropy. Tax exemption for gifts made to charity is perhaps the most obvious. In the United States, tax exemption for philanthropic gifts is a historic tradition; in Japan, it is a new experiment. A host of other incentives can be employed to reward and support private "non-governmental organizations," or NGOs. Most governments recognize the value of NGOs to the disadvantaged population. Indeed, the NGOs are the lifeblood of many developing nations, converting donations into services and administering international aid and relief.

Sometimes governments rely on NGOs to do the whole job for them. But there are even more situations in which governments attempt to guide and control the substance and form of public endeavor too closely. Misguided governments occasionally try to use NGOs and their services to fill in gaps left by their inconsistency or corruption. To be most effective, the nonprofit sector must be free to use its resources as it sees fit, independently assessing needs and attempting to meet them in its own unique way.

Governments sometimes become suspicious of foreign aid. Relief supplies funnelled into a war-torn region can end up in unintended hands; peasants in a struggling socialist country may be influenced by relief sent by a democratic nation. Medical and religious volunteers, missionaries, or technologists may be viewed as a security threat by an edgy regime. Any form of educational support, be it domestic or foreign, will be carefully scrutinized by insecure or suspicious governments. International organizations may even be forbidden to bring relief to a starving ethnic or political group because the government's design is to starve the group to death or force them to become refugees. In such settings it is difficult for any form of philanthropy to serve peoples' needs.

Philanthropy has occasionally been politicized by well-meaning citizens, foreign governments, and international religious movements. In countries where the heavy hand of government control is everywhere, many spontaneous reactions to urgent needs are stifled. Both contributions and volunteer activity are carefully controlled or discouraged.

People who live in truly democratic nations are fortunate to be able to share and give with little or no interference from the government. While human rights issues and environmental conflicts are sometimes problematic even in the freest nations, we in the United States are generally free to pursue whatever causes we believe in.

Influence of Economics

If religion is the mother of philanthropy, economics is a close member of the family. While great feats have been accomplished with little more than modest personal gifts and volunteer labor, most philanthropy involves substantial amounts of money, and so is influenced by economic conditions. America has a fundamentally sound economy in which more than 90% of our able-bodied citizens are employed. The peaks and troughs of the economic cycle have not had a long-lasting impact since World War II. There have been declines in a number of industries, but most economic change has been accompanied by some form of economic remedy. And because the American economy is relatively stable, though sometimes sluggish, American giving has increased every year for the last thirty years.

In many nations the relatively steady American economy and relatively high standard of living is deeply envied. Economic downturns and financial upheavals that would paralyze Americans if they occurred here regularly afflict many nations. Fickle world demand for various commodities, natural disasters such as flood and drought, and runaway inflation turn millions of people into paupers overnight. Shifts in demand for raw materials leave entire populations destitute and anxious to migrate.

All of these factors influence the willingness of a people to share resources with disadvantaged neighbors. Giving and volunteer activity are almost impossible when entire families have to work six days a week simply to put food on the table. There is little time to help anyone except, perhaps, family members. As the economic climate worsens, people have less to give, are less inclined to be generous to those people outside their family or community, have little time to volunteer, and are unlikely to consider the needs of other parts of their own country, much less foreign nations. Where the economy has collapsed, most financial generosity simply evaporates except on the part of the very wealthy. Even the government cannot provide services when there is little revenue. And this situation is far more common than you might think.

An energetic philanthropic system can bring about great changes in living standards, education, and health. When a nation has valuable resources, a sound economy, and a growing national output, that nation can raise funds to help eliminate illiteracy and lower infant mortality. Orphanages can be built, technical assistance can be provided to improve agriculture, cottage industries can be encouraged. And human rights problems can be investigated and remedied.

A healthy business climate spurs all sectors of a nation. NGOs can help bring about self-sufficiency in distressed areas; education liberates millions from drudgery; and governments can afford to provide services to increase the standard of living of the entire population. In a healthy economy, optimism and energy abound.

Cultural Values

One simple but powerful example of how cultural values affect philanthropy can be seen in Western Europe, where religion and philosophy have long emphasized service, charity, and compassion. For hundreds of years, benevolent acts have been encouraged and admired and social responsibility has been taught in classrooms and within the family. When millions of Europeans emigrated to the United States, they brought these traditions with them. The American philanthropic tradition owes an extraordinary debt to Western European religious and cultural values that encourage brotherhood, sharing, and private response to the needs of the disadvantaged.

In Africa, cultural values are quite different and lead to a different flow of philanthropy and good deeds. The local village or tribe commands and nurtures loyalty. Commitment to family and extended family are prevalent; a more universal view of human need and suffering is not. This narrower approach is helpful for the survival and preservation of tribal groups but does little to support a broader effort.

In Asia, the recent economic growth and dominant commercial stature of Japan, Korea, and the Republic of China have created a shift in cultural values. In much of Asia, the great new wealth is largely controlled by corporations. And a sense of corporate responsibility for the public welfare is growing, particularly in Japan. With the emergence of these highly productive nations as world entrepreneurs, the state of world philanthropy is beginning to shift. These Far East nations are more willing to aid disadvantaged countries and to contribute to domestic organizations working to bring about a better standard of living, education, and human rights for all.

Pressures are Mounting

So many paths that wind and wind,
While just the art of being kind,
Is all the sad world needs.
Ella Wheeler Wilcox

Resources and People

The world is in trouble. Economic, social and ecological systems can no longer keep pace with changes in the global situation. Dozens of world issues increase in scope and severity while our capacity to deal with them seems to diminish.

Years ago U Thant, Secretary General of the United Nations, said, "The members of the United Nations have perhaps ten years left in which to subordinate their ancient quarrels and launch a global partnership to curb the arms race, improve the human environment, defuse the population explosion, and supply the required momentum to development efforts. If such a global partnership is not forged . . . then I very much fear that the problems I have mentioned will have reached such staggering proportions that they will be beyond our capacity to control."

More than ten years have passed, and we still seem incapable of rising above our differences. War, civil war, and revolution ravage nations and cripple what tenuous progress has been made. International forums that exist to resolve disputes are rarely used. Lebanon, Iran, Iraq, Vietnam, Kampuchea, El Salvador, Ethiopia, Sudan, Somalia, and Bangladesh all suffer social, economic, and ecological devastation; their citizens are enslaved, driven out, or reduced to mere survival. Ten or twenty years of progress is callously wiped out by war. Strife, conquest, and plunder seem almost genetic in origin.

The superpowers and other developed nations spend staggering proportions of their tax revenues to support their war machines. Think of the good that could be done if what is spent on the military were redirected to social and environmental problems. But fears—both real and illusory—and the delusions of might and power keep defeating this potential first-aid for a sick planet.

Wealth and resources are not equitably distributed throughout the world. As much as 70% of the world's wealth is concentrated in countries with less than 15% of the planet's population. This dramatic imbalance takes a heavy toll.

Some areas of the globe are more richly endowed by nature than others. Oil, gold and other precious metals, fertile soil, temperate climate, friendly weather patterns, and vital minerals bless some regions and not others. Social progress, educational advances, and a favorable population distribution favor some areas over others. These factors have created significant differences in living standards between nations. The rich get richer and the poor are often exploited.

This process is accelerating. Since the beginning of the Industrial Revolution in the late eighteenth century, raw materials and scarce resources have been found and plundered by powerful industrial nations. Recently countries with large oil deposits and advanced technological capabilities have acquired enormous wealth—which only increases the fiscal imbalance as both oil and technology are needed by poorer countries for development.

The issue of the imbalance of wealth and resources has generated a great deal of ideological and diplomatic conflict. It would be unrealistic to propose that the five wealthiest nations—Japan, the United States, Germany, Saudi Arabia, and the United Kingdom—invest 10% of their wealth in the fifty poorest nations. Yet it would take an effort of such proportions to bring about meaningful change.

Many efforts have been made to spur development, beginning with the Marshall Plan after World War II. And progress has been made, notably in Japan, Germany, France, Mexico, Korea, and the Republic of China. But many nations lack the resources, technical capability, and political stability to break the cycle of ineffective economy, revolution, war, poverty, environmental plunder, and runaway population growth.

In 1900 there were 1.6 billion people on the planet. Present estimates place world population at about 4.4 billion—in less than a century the population has nearly tripled. In the next 30 to 40 years the population will reach 8 billion people, many if not most of whom will be living in poverty. Even with government-sponsored birth control programs in populous countries such as India and China, the global birth rate has not effectively slowed.

Perhaps as many as 25 million people die from starvation and water-borne disease every year, many of them young children. UNICEF says that some 45,000 infants die from starvation every day. Clearly we are not able to provide for the vast increases in world population. And religious and cultural beliefs that oppose birth control make the problem even more difficult. Some say governments have no right to limit the freedom to reproduce. Illiteracy and poor medical care also hinder efforts at population control. And so, tragically, the key restraints on population growth in the world today are famine, disease, and war.

Many other social ills plague our planet, from war and economic devastation to racial and cultural discrimination, broad-scale violation of human rights, inadequate medical care, illiteracy and unequal access to education, inadequate housing, and corrupt and ineffective governments. And soaring birthrates are commonplace in all but the most advanced nations.

The Environment

The twentieth century has callously polluted the three basic elements that sustain life: air, water, and soil. Industrial use of raw materials, fueled by the population explosion, has laid waste to vast areas of the planet. We are in effect attacking our own biosphere, the interconnected habitat of all life on earth. Near the end of a century of indifference, we are awakening to the realization that modern civilization has created a broad range of ecological crises. We must change our behavior if we are to halt or reverse these changes. It will take time, restraint, and enormous amounts of money. Virtually every nation is guilty to some degree of ecological degradation, but the most highly industrialized nations have been the most destructive.

The ozone layer in the upper atmosphere that protects the earth and its inhabitants from the sun's ultraviolet light is being steadily eroded by industrial chemicals. Oxygen-producing forests are cut down at alarming rates, and increased carbon dioxide in the upper atmosphere has already begun the deservedly feared process of global warming. Some scientists estimate that a 1% increase in global warming will raise the height of oceans enough to inundate many cities.

Energy production continues to pour pollutants into the air we breathe, increasing the toxins in our lungs and blood. Airborne pollution creates acid rain, which is already killing lakes and rivers and threatening entire water systems if not the oceans themselves. Nutrient supplies in the water are being undermined by oil and other mineral pollutants. Ocean fish, a primary food source for millions, contain ever higher levels of mercury and other toxins. In 1974 the Ford Foundation Energy Project concluded that a point of no return would be reached in thirty to 100 years, an estimate that is probably overly optimistic. We are witnessing the chemicalization of the world.

We are also depleting and destroying the soil by over-harvesting, pollution, and inefficient use. Increased reliance on chemicals to hasten growth and enrich crops has unintended aftereffects. Erosion, floods, and drought further break down the fragile ecosystems of the poorest nations. Conservation as a worldwide movement has yet to prove effective. We have simply not yet shown enough restraint and concern to change the picture. Barry Commoner, the noted American botanist, has said, ". . . we are stealing from future generations, not just lumber and coal but the basic necessities of life: air, water and soil."

Production, manufacturing, and transportation all rely on fuels for energy. Electricity, air conditioning, and air travel consume incredible quantities of fossil fuels, which exist in finite deposits. Some experts suggest that fossil fuel reserves will be gone in 30 to 50 years, yet these fuels seem necessary for the increasing standard of living most people want.

The "green revolution" and other efforts to increase world food output have been effective but are still no match for the widespread destruction of our natural resources. As much as 90% of the world's metals are used by one third of the world's population. We are now beginning to understand the incredibly complicated interconnection of the different parts of the ecosystem—it is becoming less and less possible to plead ignorance as an excuse for environmental plunder. But people and their governments are slow to change, especially where such profitable, large-scale business interests are involved.

Most tragic of all, each abuse against the environment affects every other part of the environment. Air, water, and soil are intimately interconnected. Polluted air affects water, soil, animals, fish, and human beings alike. Water carries pollutants directly to the earth, where they form a toxic bed further aggravated by pesticides and other chemicals. All wildlife is equally at risk. Species disappear at alarming rates. In our own time we have fundamentally disrupted the ecological harmony of the planet. In our own time we have dangerously disrupted the planet's natural process. And the bill is coming due. We have taken too much.

Any hope for the future lies not in taking but in giving.

N·I·N·E

NATIONAL AND GLOBAL RESPONSE

America's Crisis

It was the best of times, it was the worst of times . . . it was the season of light, it was the season of darkness, it was the spring of hope, it was the winter of despair . . .
Charles Dickens

The opening of *A Tale of Two Cities* is as descriptive of our age as it was of Dickens's. America keeps changing, and the new needs that accompany each change aren't always immediately mirrored by new giving patterns. New problems arise with a sudden urgency, and our response to them is limited. These problems are often confounding, bewildering, and frustrating because there are no simple solutions. Awesome forces are working against efforts to provide each of us with a life of dignity, respect, love, and equality:

- Economic downturns and consequent financial insecurity.
- Reduction in government support of key social services.
- Inadequate housing for many of the nation's 35 million poor.
- Collapse of many of the nation's banks.
- Increased crime and political corruption.
- Growing hostility and distrust, and a lack of respect for life and property.

- A functionally illiterate population of 27 million people.
- A staggering high school dropout rate and bleak work prospects for dropouts.
- A sharp increase in homelessness with no clear remedy for the problem.
- Continued growth of drug addiction and alcoholism.
- A substantial increase in America's aged population and the consequent severe strain on social and medical services.
- Runaway medical and health-care costs.
- Continuation of the AIDS epidemic.
- High birth rate among the poor and underprivileged.

These are all urgent issues that need immediate attention. The private sector—foundations, corporations, and individuals—will need to provide greater assistance to nonprofit organizations struggling to relieve these social ills. We all need to become more personally involved, more generous. We need to become more responsive and sensitive to the needs of those less capable, less intelligent, less able to cope. This will be difficult, there being so many substantial barriers to greater involvement, including:

- A decline of confidence in the strength of the economy and a more survival-oriented national attitude. A resurgence of the "look out for number one" syndrome.
- A steady decline in the influence of religion, the mother of philanthropy. A 1988 Gallup poll showed that religion was considered "very important" by slightly more than one half (53%) of the population, a decline from a high of 75% in 1952.

- The negative impact of the televangelist scandals.
- The decline in the Catholic church donor base, on a per capita basis, to almost one half what it was twenty years ago.

American religious organizations are the nation's major non-government providers of human services. Many will be severely strained in the coming decade, especially facilities that provide medical care and health instruction; day care; free or low-cost meals for the elderly, indigent and homeless; counseling; housing assistance; and care for the mentally ill or dying. While religious contributions have shown a healthy increase in recent years, erosion of the large donor base, the declining influence of the church, and the decline in people's confidence in the economy may lead to decreased involvement in and support of service and educational programs.

Looking at the future, a recent blue-ribbon panel report from The American Council on Education warned, "The nation will suffer a lower standard of living, social conflict will intensify, our ability to compete in world markets will decline, our economy will falter, and our national security will be endangered."

Individual concerns that also threaten the growth of community service and philanthropy include:

- Many Americans are showing signs of discouragement and frustration with increasing social problems. Will they increase their service efforts or begin a slow retreat to indifference?
- A sense of personal isolation, fragmentation, and alienation is growing in America. Social conflict contributes to a divided and uneasy nation.
- People feel a creeping powerlessness, a lack of control over major issues such as illiteracy, sub-standard hous-

ing, drugs, crime, and homelessness. Despite the best efforts of individuals, institutions, and the government, these troubles continue to grow.

· The gulf between the affluent and the 35 million Americans who live in poverty keeps widening. This economic imbalance brings added stress to all of our social issues.

· Aside from church-related support, the average American only volunteers or contributes to one or two charities or causes. This level of support is not sufficient.

· Fear, hostility, and distrust are beginning to diminish the empathy of dedicated and generous supporters. Many are unable to determine the legitimacy and effectiveness of both new and seasoned organizations. Corruption and scandal shake people's faith and willingness to help.

And finally, at the environmental level, there are a host of afflictions that beset America, including:

· Widespread air and water pollution.
· Deforestation, strip mining, and overuse of public lands.
· Toxic waste, harmful pesticides, and inadequate waste management.
· Destruction of wildlife and endangered species.
· Noise pollution, overcrowding and allied environmental stresses.

There is much that is positive about America's response to social problems, but we certainly have our work cut out for us. These lists of woes, evils, and pressing imbalances are intended not to discourage us but to dramatize our plight and our opportunities. As a nation we have overcome great environmental and social problems in the past. Only a hundred years ago we had incredibly high infant mortality, uncontrollable epidemics, widespread child labor, gross discrimination by sex and color, outrageous exploitation of workers, unsafe drinking water, appalling sanitation, and severely limited educational opportunities. None of these evils has been eradicated, but all of them have been dramatically improved.

It is extraordinarily difficult to engineer effective social change. A single high-intensity assault upon a problem usually will not do the job. Patience and determined effort by all—particularly individual initiative—seem to produce the most enduring changes in the quality of life in America. It's all up to you and me. And since we have no direct control over each other, the responsibility for change and improvement falls on our own shoulders. When all is said and done, we hold the key to change and growth. We are the future.

The Global Ecological Disaster

Examples are few of men ruined by giving. Men are heroes in spending, cravens in what they give.
Christian Nestell Bovee

How is the world responding to the breakdown of our planet's ecology? Are we organizing to change our lives so that future generations will have a world as bountiful and as beautiful as the one we inherited? What are some of the factors that keep us from meeting this enormous challenge?

Some scientists say it is already too late for our planet, that no matter what changes we may make from now on, we have entered a "final countdown." The urgent needs of mankind for food, fuel, shelter, transportation and sheer survival seem to have taken precedence over our care for the planet.

It is easy to be lulled into a false sense of security about the environment. The predicted catastrophes have not yet overtaken us. Global warming has not yet flooded the lowlands. There have been fewer authoritative reports about increases in cancer or the destruction of plant and animal life by ultraviolet rays than we might expect. Every day it seems we hear of vast new oil reserves. And so industrial nations ignore most pollutants, trusting that the public will not be alarmed by what they cannot see or feel. For the most part pollution is an invisible enemy.

The problem is not so much that the public is indifferent or ignorant, but that government is slow-moving and that the need for profits sometimes requires industry to behave in ways damaging to the environment. Most industries know how to use fuels and other resources more efficiently. They can switch to safer processes and sources, but profit margins are larger with the older systems already in place. Automobile manufacturers can already produce cars that use alternative fuels or less gasoline. There are safer, less dangerous pesticides. Many industries can easily diminish water pollution. We can restore the environment. Forests can be replanted, erosion stopped, and sea water converted into fresh.

But these changes will cost billions and require great political courage. No multinational corporation willingly faces a drop in profits. No population willingly taxes itself. So we pass on our responsibilities to the next generation and rationalize our delay by saying that the negative effects on the environment are in dispute, that our existing social problems demand our full attention, and that the richer countries cannot afford to do more because of their own pressing problems.

And all of this is true. Even our most pressing problems—famine, war, AIDS—are not being well handled. Most nations are poor in resources and in literacy. Debtor nations whose economic, political, and environmental systems are extremely fragile lack the ability to tackle even their own most significant problems, let alone global issues. In fact, most of the nations of the world have such distressing internal problems that they cannot begin to lighten the burden of their suffering neighbors.

Survival and the development of an export economy are far more urgent issues for developing nations than their own ecosystems. These nations justify ravages of nature by the need to improve their tragic domestic situations. They may be concerned about damage to the biosphere and global warming, about the survival of whales and buffalo, but they have been forced to forego concern about most environmental issues simply to survive. When urged to try conservation measures, they are often coached by technologists from the very countries that depleted their resources in the first place.

Most nations and peoples have no clear concept of stewardship of the earth. The disadvantaged nations are limited by their struggle for survival and self-sufficiency and, often, by the ignorance of their populations. The advanced nations know that the burden of change rests on them, both to aid the poorer nations and to save the environment.

But the burden is too great. Progress is made, but the population explosion, wars, pestilence, and environmental ills keep accelerating. Even strong nations can be overwhelmed.

Moreover, there is no credible blueprint for transformation of the environment. The simultaneous resolution of social problems and restoration of the ecological system seem beyond our capacity even to plan, let alone accomplish. And no real progress can be made until the public understands both the problem and its solutions. Until then, we will never agree to dismantle and replace much of the world's energy, transportation, and industrial structure, which is what it could take to transform the way we use land, fuel, and other natural resources.

Although we are beginning to cooperate internationally on critical issues like arms control, most nations are still primarily occupied with internal stresses. A 1987 study of well-educated and affluent Americans by the Overseas Development Council found that two out of three Americans think we need to solve our own poverty problems before we look to problems abroad. This attitude clearly limits our ability to act globally.

Two Scenarios for the Year 2000

> If you want to innovate, to change an enterprise or a society, it takes people willing to do what's not expected.
>
> *Jean Riboud*

The effort we make in the next few years to resolve our most pressing social ills will set the stage for the next century. As troubles multiply, each of us needs to volunteer, contribute, and advocate to bring about change. Even if we personally may have had little to do with the creation of these troubles, we are called upon nonetheless to solve them.

As a nation we have drifted toward serious dysfunction for years. National and global problems have accelerated at a time when the government and the business community have been unable to marshal enough resources to help. We have made progress in some areas but in others our efforts have been about as effective as a bandaid on a gunshot wound. Every one of us will be needed if we are to reverse the deterioration all around us. The issues are broad in scope, and our responses need to be imaginative and all-encompassing. What we as individuals do—how we react and how we commit ourselves—is critical. Millions of people have been deeply committed and heavily involved for years, but if the problems are to be finally solved, it will take millions more of us in the future from all over the world.

I have constructed two possible scenarios for the results of our efforts as we finish this century.

Scenario #1—Into the Darkness

- Governments reduce funding for major programs and eliminate support for many small but deserving programs. Numerous environmental programs are dismantled and their funds used to prop up deteriorating health, housing, and education projects.
- An economic downturn forces many businesses to sharply reduce or eliminate their charitable contributions. Firms pull back from community support in response to a profit-oriented managerial philosophy.
- An economically depressed and financially anxious population reduces its contributions to religious institutions, forcing churches to curtail vital support services.
- Individualism and self-interest erode the effectiveness of nonprofit organizations as staff members struggle fiercely to save their own favorite program—and their jobs. Leadership falters and effectiveness disintegrates.
- Organizational insecurity and chaos spill over into the volunteer ranks where frustration, confusion, and par-

tisan responses destroy cooperation. The people who continue to serve form protective, fragmented groups that jealously guard their own turf.

- Volunteers and donors become disheartened and pull back from their commitments, which further reduces both morale and the funds available for services. Budget battles escalate as professionals scramble for a place on the ark.
- The recipients of community services, poorly served, become increasingly resentful, suspicious, and uncooperative.

In this picture each setback feeds on the others, plunging the system of volunteer effort and spontaneous giving into chaos. As exaggerated as such a scenario may seem, it is possible. When the government pulls back and the economy falters, all of these conditions can arise. It's true that past recessions did not materially affect giving in America, but the need for services and problems with the environment are growing at a dizzying pace while the economy, saddled with debt and dislocations, is not. There are indications that it will take years for the nation to overcome the financial excesses of the 1980s.

Despite all governmental and economic predictions, the vitality of the nonprofit world and the effectiveness of service programs will be most influenced by what individuals do. It all filters down to the scope and intensity of my commitment to my neighbor, your commitment to yours. If we believe in the extended benefits of giving and volunteering and act on these beliefs, then we can avoid this first chaotic scenario.

Scenario #2—Into the Light

Healthy and effectively functioning philanthropy in the future will require:

- An economy that is manageable and able to cope with financial stresses. Runaway inflation and collapse are avoided as enlightened cooperation outpaces greed.
- A long-term commitment to critical services and environmental programs on the part of the government. Rather than shift priorities at whim, the government steadily maintains funding and manpower for key programs.
- A population that has faith in the power and necessity of giving and volunteering. Enough faith to willingly set aside at least five hours per week for community service, and five percent of income for gifts.
- A citizenry that does not feel insecure or impoverished when making large gifts.
- A society of individuals who can cooperate with their neighbors on a sustained basis for the public good.
- People who select volunteer assignments to maximize their enjoyment.
- Religious teaching that focuses on brotherhood and is put into practice.
- An educational system that instructs and involves young people in community service. Service should be made part of the school curriculum to equip our young people to help disadvantaged neighbors.
- A government that uses public information and legislation to promote volunteer involvement. In education, government funding can be designed to establish more public service and nonprofit opportunities.

Having described these two possibilities, it would be unfair to end this section without sharing some thoughts on how you personally might go about ensuring the second. I can think of no person more qualified to help with this task than the psychiatrist and humanist M. Scott Peck. In his book *The Different Drum*, Dr. Peck eloquently describes steps and actions we might consider.

The reality is that we are inevitably social creatures who desperately need each other, not merely for sustenance, not merely for company, but for any meaning to our lives whatsoever. These then are the seeds from which community can grow.

Peck endorses Alexis de Tocqueville, who in 1835 said the one characteristic that most impressed him about Americans was our individualism. De Tocqueville warned, however, that unless our individualism was balanced by other habits, it would lead to the fragmentation of American society and the social isolation of its citizens. To counterbalance that individualism, Peck urges us all to "Start communities. Start one in your church. Start one in your school. Start one in your neighborhood."

Peck quotes the early Pilgrim leader John Winthrop, who described some of the major dimensions of "community":

We must delight in each other, make others' conditions our own, rejoice together, mourn together, labor and suffer together, always having before our eyes our community as members of the same body.

Peck goes on to encourage us all:

Start your own community. It won't be easy. You will be scared. You will often feel that you don't know what you're doing. You will have a difficult time persuading people to join you. Many initially won't want to make the commitment . . . Once you get started it will be frustrating. But hang in there. Push forward into emptiness. It will be painful . . . Don't stop halfway. It may seem like dying but push on. And then suddenly you will find yourself in the clean air of the mountaintop and you'll be laughing and crying and feeling more alive than you have in years—maybe more alive than you've ever been.

> So start community. Don't be afraid to fail . . . True
> community is always, among other things, an adven-
> ture . . . and you will be able to share not only your fear
> but your talents and strengths. Out of the strength of
> your community you will be able to do things you never
> thought you were capable of.

These inspirational words offer both encouragement
and direction. They could become a rallying cry as we
lead ourselves into the light. That is my hope—I trust it is
yours as well.

T · E · N

VOLUNTEERS
FOR THE PLANET

Communication is the Key

Each time a man stands up for an ideal, or acts to improve the lot of others, or strikes out against injustice, he sends forth a tiny ripple of hope.

Robert F. Kennedy

All relationships rely on communication. In business and in government, goals cannot be met without being properly defined through precise communication. Successful communication brings meaning and fosters understanding in any endeavor. Where communication isn't effective, it blunts opportunities for people to succeed in causes that are important to them.

Nowhere is good communication more important than in philanthropy and volunteering. Organizations that depend on donations and a corps of volunteers—nonprofit organizations—need even more sensitive and precise communication than do businesses. According to Dr. John Haggai, there is always the danger that "worthy thoughts were not given a chance because they were not presented worthily."

The role of communication in philanthropy is a complex one. Communication can be an appeal for financial support or a recruitment plea. It can be a description of services offered, goals to be achieved, or tasks to be accomplished. Some of the purposes of communication in philanthropy are:

- Promoting the benefits and rewards of giving and volunteering.
- Requesting funds, help, and advocacy in a spirit of sharing.
- Describing the needs and the mission of the organization.
- Matching people to challenging, satisfying assignments.
- Praising, acknowledging, and thanking donors and volunteers for their contributions.
- Campaigning to retain veteran volunteers and long-standing donors.
- Urging advocates to carry the message to legislators, government, and the public.
- Mounting special promotions to attract young people to community service.
- Lobbying for educational involvement in teaching about, encouraging, and sponsoring community service.
- Mounting campaigns to urge college graduates to choose community service careers.
- Creating and promoting service opportunities that will challenge and reward students.
- Developing television programming that will teach elementary school children the benefits of community service and altruism.
- Soliciting and listening to feedback from donors and volunteers.
- Publicizing and praising the efforts of volunteers in much the same way that President Bush promotes his

"Thousand Points of Light." Establishing a data bank of good deeds that the media can draw on, and encouraging them to do so.

- Conveying the organization's plans and problems to donors, volunteers, and staff.
- Holding brainstorming sessions to develop more effective and efficient programs, fund appeals, and advocacy strategies.
- Singling out energetic and active volunteers, donors, and advocates for special recognition and publicity.
- Selectively and efficiently setting forth the challenges and benefits of giving for prime donor prospects.
- Promoting the organization's programs to potential clients.
- Enlisting former clients in volunteer activities.
- Soliciting advice, input, and feedback from clients.

Take a moment to review this list. Your cause or religious institution might benefit if you would undertake some of these communication tasks. There is plenty to communicate, and often staff personnel are too overworked to handle the job. Perhaps you can help them or know someone else who can. Keep in mind that the most important communication of all is the tribute that you as a volunteer pay to the people who benefit from your program by showing up and sharing with them. By this all-important act you tell them that they and the cause are valued.

Making a Difference Globally

It's not the difference between people that's the difficulty. It's the indifference.

Anonymous

The forces that drive nations are complex and shifting, and events and conditions seldom remain constant. So to suggest specific solutions to improve philanthropic activity around the world is a complex exercise and well beyond the scope of this book. Instead I would like to focus on what concerned Americans can do to meet the challenges of human need and ecological imbalance abroad, and to highlight some of the opportunities to make a difference we have here at home.

Take disaster and famine relief programs, for instance. To help in these emergencies there are at least seven possible approaches:

- Donate money and resources to international relief organizations such as Care, UNICEF, the Interfaith Hunger Fund, Catholic Relief Services, Joint Jewish Distribution Committee, Save the Children, Church World Service, and World Concern. I have served all of these agencies in one form or another as a consultant during the past twenty-five years and I can testify to their integrity and effectiveness. The Interfaith Hunger Fund, in fact, was born in my New York offices several years ago.
- Become involved in fund-raising for one of these organizations. Become a volunteer or start your own grassroots solicitation of money, food, or clothing.
- Lobby the government to increase assistance to poorer countries. Help sway public opinion in favor of assistance. Write your congressmen and senators. Be an activist.
- Involve your friends in your project. Ask them to help you lobby and raise funds.
- Help local media inform the public about your cause.
- Think about specific ways to aid disadvantaged countries. One volunteer convinced a water-pump man-

ufacturer to donate pumps and send technical advisors to a disaster area. You might canvass local manufacturers seeking gifts in kind.

· Provide information to schools and youth groups. Become a spokesperson for your cause and enlist the support of concerned young people. Numerous studies of young adults suggest that they are eager to volunteer if someone asks them and sets up a structure that makes it easy for them to become involved.

Many of these strategies can be used for other pressing issues, such as human rights violations, the elimination of illiteracy, the rebuilding of a distressed ecosystem, or flood relief. The emphasis may shift to political action, lobbying and advocacy, or to the raising of funds for technical assistance. But the principles are much the same for any effort to generate support for international crises.

Though we may never visit a disadvantaged country or see the problems firsthand, we can still take steps to help people in some needy country. Each of us has some capability. We can prepare press releases, assist at special events, enlist volunteers, lobby with legislators, appeal to corporations to become sponsors, or simply tell our friends about our concern and ask them to support it as well. All these efforts can help solve these global problems while bringing a new sense of joy and meaning to our lives.

Emergence of Global Responsibility

It seems obvious that before the end of the century we must accomplish basic changes in our relations with ourselves and with nature. If this is to be done, we must begin now.

M.I.T. *Study of Critical Environmental Problems*

We live in a time of disaster when one crisis follows another. As soon as we put out one fire, another more threatening one starts. And if nations are busy responding to the hottest flame, the most dangerous social evil, the most destructive war, they cannot take adequate measures to roll back the tide of social and ecological devastation.

And yet there are ways you can help the slow process of remedying global social and environmental imbalances. There will be no quick fixes—the problems are immense and deeply rooted. But each of us has resources that can be used to help create a more peaceful, secure, healthy planet. We sometimes feel powerless, confused, and overwhelmed, but we are not without talent and the capacity to bring about valuable changes.

First, you must realize that it is up to you as an individual to start healing the planet. The responsibility rests squarely on your shoulders and on mine. You don't need to make a grand gesture—to sell all your property, donate the proceeds, and join the Peace Corps. But you can take simple steps that can be enlarged by neighbors and fellow workers.

To begin with, you can learn more about environmental crises and suggested remedies. Read books on proposals to rescue the planet—but be sure they are recent, as the environmental field changes constantly. Second, stop using environmentally dangerous products such as pesticides, plastics, and aerosol cans. As a consumer you have countless opportunities to vote against a company's policies of neglect—don't buy their products. Boycott indifferent manufacturers. Often the press will report on firms that are illegally dumping toxic waste and ruining the soil. Support legislation for greater monitoring and controls on pollution. Write your congressmen, educate your neighbors, write to the press, become a crusader against institutions that violate the environment. Advocate more stringent restrictions, more complete conservation, and the elimination of toxic manufacturing processes.

And keep in mind that as you get into the battle to save the planet, you will be going up against the forces of environmental exploitation. They are formidable foes and will resist any efforts to make them correct their excesses. The fight won't be easy.

Of course, you don't have to do battle alone. There are friends of the earth everywhere making their voices heard in state capitals, Congress, and throughout the world. Join with other concerned citizens of the world who study environmental problems. Participate in rallies, demonstrations, and efforts to acquaint the voting public with local or national polluters. Encourage the governmental awareness of environmental excesses and pollution of the air and water. If you can, give to organizations involved in saving the environment. Volunteer to work with them locally. Find opportunities to make a difference and jump in with both feet.

The world's social ills are daunting, but there is still much you can personally do to help. Start with a simple review of the needs that touch you most, the ones for which you have the most empathy. To some, local community issues will be most important. To others, national and international illiteracy and poverty may be uppermost. You may be one who tries to balance local activity with financial or advocacy assistance for international catastrophes or natural disasters. There are many more needs than we can ever possibly fill, which makes it important to help the causes you most believe in and that can give you a sense of satisfaction when progress is made. Move toward those that strike a responsive chord. Show your support by:

- Volunteering to serve the cause as a fund raiser.
- Making a contribution to your organization.
- Lobbying and advocating for the cause.
- Giving food, property, or income to your organization.
- Volunteering your talents and services to help others in need throughout the world.

Certain causes may hold a special interest for you. You may decide to lobby, write letters, demonstrate, educate the public, or convey your views to local or national legislators. Do what Howard and Connie Clery did. Work to have new legislation passed by Congress. Work to elect legislators who favor your stands on the social issues that most concern you.

All of these ways of expressing your concern and compassion are likely to be available through your local church or religious institution. Join your talents and support to theirs, on behalf of the causes you care about.

In *No World Without End*, Katherine and Peter Montague issue this challenge: ". . . across the land small groups of citizens have been and still are working in their various ways to provide a world of economic justice; clean air and water; uncontaminated soils; safe supplies of energy; safe, convenient, efficient, and low-cost public transportation; . . . clean, quiet and safe streets; . . . thriving small town and regional economies; adequate child care facilities; inexpensive and humane health care; decent housing for all; easily accessible education services; widely available legal help; justice in the courts; clean work places, and meaningful work for all."

You can join them.

E·L·E·V·E·N

ACTING FOR THE FUTURE

Making A Difference

Where there is no vision, the people perish.

Proverbs 29:18

The greatest barrier to improving society and the environment is indifference. So many people, absorbed with their own needs and immediate problems, do not see that all of us ultimately are affected when any one of us suffers. Children are sensitive to others around them, but as we grow older many of us become progressively more selfish. We don't lose our compassion and concern entirely, but often they are pushed aside by ambition, acquisitiveness, or sometimes the sheer need to survive in our demanding, pressurized society. If we are sufficiently troubled about the future, the resulting fear eventually breeds insensitivity. We lose perspective, to the point that all our energy and thoughts are for ourselves, not for others.

The same dynamic also operates in governments and nations. In a world of crises, fear and self-interest can be absolutely blinding. We try to deal with pressing issues through politics and organizations, through economic readjustment, self-sufficiency programs, and reforms. But while a government or its citizens concentrate on one crisis, three or four other crises grow in urgency. Revolution, reform, massive government aid, and the intense efforts of millions of dedicated people bring only limited—or fleeting—success.

The problems of the planet are far from resolved. Most grow more intense by the day, while the people who struggle with the degradation of the environment, human rights, famine, illiteracy, poverty, drug abuse, and homelessness grow weary and disillusioned. Others, who march to the drumbeat of self-serving contemporary values, don't see the meaning in philanthropic activities. Their indifference is profound.

We need to promote change if we are to emerge from the endless cycle of global conflicts and disasters. These changes cannot begin with governments, national leaders, or large multinational organizations; they must begin with you and me. John D. Rockefeller III put it very well in his book about philanthropy, *The Second American Revolution*: "The essence of private initiative is the decision by individuals to become involved and committed to something larger than themselves." And as I've said, through consistent sharing and caring for something larger than ourselves, we can become physically, emotionally, and spiritually whole. What an exciting possibility for each of us! We commit to changing the world and we get changed for the better in the process.

To counter global catastrophes we need many resources. And the most essential resource is committed and responsive individuals, individuals who will live by the concluding words of the Declaration of Independence: ". . . we mutually pledge to each other our lives, our fortunes, and our sacred honor." You and I are the most important resource in the struggle to save our planet.

Change and growth can occur only when each of us accepts the truth that *we must all give of ourselves so that we all may live*. Transformation begins when we change our attitude and our actions. The effects of the fully committed few have only begun to stem the rising tide of social, political, and environmental problems. More and more of us must join them. More and more of us must learn how to give to live on this planet.

We have reached a stage where we cannot leave this work solely to institutions, governments, or leaders. In fact, we are living in a fool's paradise if we expect them to resolve our problems. When you hear over and over, "It's up to you. You are the only one who can do it. You are all mankind," your reaction may be, "I'm no miracle worker. The troubles in the community, nation, world, are just too enormous, too complex." Well, that's the point.

You are the miracle worker—*without your efforts there will be no miracle*. At some level deep inside, you probably understand this. Naturally, you don't want to inherit the problems of the world, especially when you probably aren't directly guilty of anything more damaging than a little pollution. Yet, like it or not, the problems of the world are yours and will only get worse if you turn your back on them. You don't need another bundle of troubles, but that's the nature of social and environmental responsibility.

Each of us needs to accept a new mission. We cannot heal all of the problems of the earth by ourselves, but we have to believe that if enough of us commit ourselves and turn loose our energies and resources, collectively we can create wholeness. When an out-of-work rock musician, Bob Geldof, had the idea for musical support to hungry Africans, he couldn't foresee that his Band-Aid album and Live Aid concerts would net $83 million in relief funds. All he had was a vision and the commitment to act on it. You don't know how much of a contribution you can make until you start. You can energize yourself, go beyond your present limits, and change the world.

Once you decide you are ready to go the extra mile, you will need to reallocate your time, energy, and talents.

More than one philosopher has said that the renewal of society and our planet must begin with a single individual—not the collective power of governments and organizations but the responsible, committed, caring individual. Progress and change live only in the mind and the hearts of committed, compassionate citizens.

Perhaps you are trying to give some personal dimensions to this commitment. Given the resources you have, you might wonder how your efforts could have anything but the most limited impact. The truth is that you have many resources you may not be aware of:

- Your energy and willingness to become involved.
- Your valuable time.
- Your talents, knowledge, and abilities.
- Your ideas and visions of a better world.
- Your compassion and concern for others.
- Your financial resources.
- Your commitment to use all of these to make a difference.

Given these essential building blocks, each of us can launch a program to begin changing conditions. The way to start is with baby steps, simple inquiries into whatever mission might best fit our talents and circumstances. Since many of us already volunteer, our commitment may simply mean greater involvement. None of this requires a grand entrance or great pronouncements; just a deep, perhaps visceral recognition that we will need to invest a little extra effort, expend a few more hours a week, or give more generously.

Remember that any commitment you make is really with yourself. It can take whatever form you like but it needs to be freely made to be fully realized. Don't get involved just to please a relative or friend, though this may be the initial impetus. Once you accept the reality that a better world begins with you, relax in the knowledge that you will be the beneficiary of wonderfully rich, life-sustaining experiences. Your journey will not lead you down a road of sacrifice and drudgery. With grace and perseverance, you'll get much more than you give.

How to Begin: An Example

> Individuals . . . alone can make the decision to become involved, and . . . if they do not, they miss their most important chance to feel a sense of inner power, to become whole human beings.
>
> *John D. Rockefeller III*

Once you have decided where you would like to take a stand for a better planet, you can begin tapping into a whole medley of resources. To look at some of them, let's return to the example of eliminating illiteracy in Cleveland, Ohio. Assume that this project vitally interests you.

Your first step is to discover how much illiteracy there is and what programs already exist to combat it. Start by contacting the government, social services organizations, the Cleveland Board of Education, the United Way, and local foundations. Your aim is to educate yourself. You may have some well-formed ideas about illiteracy and how you would like to help, but you still need to get a briefing about the extent of the issue and what is already being done to correct it. The more information you have, the better the chances are that you can help.

Once you see the big picture, you may see a role for yourself. You may, for example, discover that there is a well-organized and comprehensive program for young children and high school dropouts but no programs for illiterates in the workplace, whether American adults with no schooling or people whose native language is not English.

At this point you may feel enthusiastic about a project to help illiterate adult Americans. What you need now is support, guidance, funding, teachers, pupils, classrooms, and promotion. Perhaps you also need city approval of classroom materials. So you make up a list of what you think you need. Then, once you've gotten by the sinking feeling that what you are trying to do is impossible, get in touch with people who might help you. These might include:

Education Experts

- Cleveland Board of Education
- State Board of Education
- U.S. Department of Health, Education, and Welfare
- Local teachers' union or council
- Retired teachers' association

From this group you are seeking guidance, contacts, potential teachers, used books, and suggested curricula.

Government Leaders

- Cleveland social services directors
- Mayor's office
- Housing, transportation offices
- State officials, senators, representatives
- Federal Officers, congressmen, senators

These can provide program funding, classrooms, books, supplies, even information about which business establishments may have illiterate workers.

Funding Sources

- Local United Way
- Local and regional foundations interested in education
- Local universities and private schools
- Church groups
- Government grants
- Local businesses large and small
- Concerned citizens, friends, neighbors

Once you have done some planning and enlisted others in the project, you need a budget. It should estimate the cost of classroom rental, books, supplies, a central information office, phones, publicity, and transportation. You can build a volunteer teaching staff and use empty classrooms at night or on the weekend.

The Business Community

- Large and small manufacturers
- Service organizations
- Business groups, like the Better Business Bureau
- Labor unions

Virtually every local firm is a potential source of financial support and of people in need of education. In large organizations you can get in touch with the human resources manager or Employee Assistance Program for contributions and publicity. Greater literacy will benefit industry as well as individuals, so don't be shy about asking businesses for help.

The Media

- Local daily and weekly newspapers
- Local television and radio stations
- Local or regional magazines
- Business and social service newsletters

The media can be a valuable partner in your efforts, publicizing your program and class schedules. But make sure you tailor your publicity to the people you are trying to reach. In this case your prime audience does not read English, so you need to gear your publicity to literate relatives, friends, and co-workers who'll be able to carry the message for you. Your should use every source available to you at little or no cost. Bear in mind, your advertisements may qualify as public service announcements. The media can help you raise funds by doing human interest stories about your efforts.

Volunteer Teaching Staff

- Local colleges and universities (faculty and students)
- Public school teachers
- Retired or former school teachers
- Retired professional people
- Active professional people
- Church group members

You may find that recruiting a teaching staff is easier than attracting pupils. For many there is a sense of shame over illiteracy. To some extent, your printed invitation may need to be directed at concerned family members and acquaintances, urging them to inform illiterate friends and relatives.

Whatever cause or organization you choose, remember that there are many resources that can be enlisted and cultivated in your efforts to bring about change. Using them effectively requires ingenuity and perseverance. And don't underestimate the desire of others to help when they see something good happening. Programs that are accomplishing something have a way of attracting support from the most improbable sources. To expand your role you have to become a "town crier," publicizing the cause of literacy whenever and wherever you can. Become a walking conversation about your project. Enlist everyone you can.

You'll be amazed at how many resources become available once you go into action.

The Global Horizon

If we are to lift ourselves out of this morass, we must shift our sights from the superficial to the sacrificial.
Jesse Jackson

Our global focus has become clouded and our vision obscured. In the past, war and revolution have been the principal means of resolving conflict. We have not done a very good job of understanding other human beings. As long as our concern includes only our own race, country, community, religion, or family we will continue to live in a turbulent world. But once we see that there is a possibility of living happily and safely together on the earth, we can start building a new unified world.

Nationalism, ethnic and religious prejudice, and closed or exclusive affiliations divide us. Under their influence we can hate, violate human rights, punish others economically, even go to war—and feel good about it. Despite international forums like the United Nations, we still are not always able to reason together peaceably.

There are some elements in our society trying to teach nations to restrain themselves. Most religions urge us to mediate disputes rather than take up arms against each other. But nationalistic spirit largely dictates global policy, and nationalist fervor is sometimes fanned by religious leaders who misinterpret the teachings of their community. Discrimination occurs at all levels.

Some nations become more self-enclosing and protective. A universal or global mind set is emerging, but there are dozens of nations and millions of nationalistic citizens who prefer to dwell upon differences rather than focus on similarities and cooperative opportunities. Much of this has to do with economic and political power. Degradation of ecosystems, pollution, and exploitation of the poor are too often byproducts of the efforts of multinational corporations to extend their markets, increase production, or promote consumption of toxic products.

Human beings create governments to keep themselves safe. Often, in attempts to maintain an ideology or preserve a lifestyle, these governments can oppress or disenfranchise millions. In many parts of the world human life has little sanctity or value—a reality that is unlikely to change much in the near future unless we shift our focus. For centuries nations have proclaimed the sanctity of the individual citizen and then enslaved, banished, or exploited them. Oppression, economic greed, corruption, suppression of human rights, and plundering of the environment are, unfortunately, the norm in our global society.

I don't know any grand solutions to the complex and ever-expanding array of global disturbances. I do know that we need to change our focus. For too long national governments have been the central players in global deterioration. In the interest of security, economic advancement, cultural and ethnic survival, we have given governments great powers. As a result, the individual has abandoned or relinquished much personal power. In many nations, individual power has been taken away by dictatorial government—with disastrous results.

Most governments function ineffectively, some destructively. We have all seen the proliferation in various countries of government programs that favor the rich, the powerful, and the warlike. If the billions spent for defense by the nations of the world were redirected to social programs, hunger, disease, poverty and illiteracy would end. As a nation and as a member of the global community, our own country has had—still has—the resources to transform our hungry, impoverished, troubled world.

Since World War II we as a nation have chosen to focus great resources on war and communist encroachment in the name of "protecting our way of life." Protection it may have been, but at what cost? We might have established an adequate protection for perhaps one half of the billions we allocated to defense. We saw Vietnam as an enormous threat and we overreacted. Instead of using our resources to improve life and heal the planet, we spent hundreds of billions to wreak havoc and destruction . . . and we divided our own nation.

Understand, I am not against military action, though I am against wars of aggression as a means of resolving problems. While I was working on the manuscript for this book, America, along with an international coalition, went to war to wrest Kuwait from Iraqi control. And I believe that our decision to do so, when months of negotiation were to no avail was just and right.

Now that the war is over and the coalition has won, we have a unique opportunity to show our commitment to environmental issues. I like the idea Edwin Dillard, a seventy-seven-year-old retiree in Greenville, Tennessee, expressed in a letter to his local newspaper:

"Experts said it would take months, perhaps years, to drive Saddam Hussein out of Kuwait in a ground war. Now they're saying it could take several years to put out the oil wells burning across the country he was actually driven out of in a little less than four days.

"Why not turn the troops and equipment—and ingenuity—already over there against the massive oil spill and devastating well fires Hussein has unleashed in the world? Couldn't the bombers that are already there be loaded with high explosives (or cement, or sand) and sent against the fires? I don't know whether such an effort would be practicable or if it would work in the end, but I think it's important to try anyway. We need to show we care as much about the environment as we do about containing aggression. We need to find our sense of proportion."

We certainly haven't found this proportion in the past. The thing that disturbs me most about the huge military budget is that it virtually ensures no meaningful progress will be made in the war on poverty, inadequate health care, illiteracy, crime, drug addiction, and the other social ills that beset us. I'm convinced that we have had the focus on the wrong set of issues. There has to be a more responsible way than war to resolve nationalistic disputes and acts of naked aggression. These issues are exceedingly complex and provoke intense feelings, and I don't see many short-term solutions on the horizon.

I want to suggest, though, that a way to start is to plan. I propose a major planning effort, at both the national level to reorder our domestic priorities and at the international level to deal with the monumental problems of disadvantaged nations and global environmental threats.

If we are to survive and progress, we need to alter our priorities drastically or we will surely see even greater domestic unrest, human suffering, and environmental collapse. We cannot forever postpone or hastily patch the cracks in the dam. These are my suggestions. I hope they are worth promoting.

- We should review and prioritize all the major social and environmental issues at the national and international level.

- We should give the highest priority to the preservation of life, protection of health, provision for shelter, and protection of human rights. All nations—starting with our own—must hold these as inalienable rights.

- We must be willing to support the programs that have been given priority. Once elective bodies have established priorities, we need to act in concert to implement them. Our government raises funds in order to execute programs as *we*, the people, direct.

- We need to learn everything we can about the extent of our social and environmental ills and the cost of correcting them. With this knowledge we can petition others and the government to develop and fund needed programs. This requires public education to inform us all about the severity of our social and environmental troubles and what *each one of us* can do to help overcome them. Americans *can* move from entrenched self-interest to massive self-help and support.

- Power needs to be rooted at the level of the individual. We need to understand that we have adequate resources to destroy the roots of poverty. During the Depression and World War II, we were a nation in crisis and we triumphed. We can do it again. We can harness both the powers of our government and our own personal powers.

· To establish sensible social programs that the whole nation will endorse, we need to be willing to endure adjustments and sacrifices. We might, for example, consider a more progressive distribution of wealth tied to work effort and taxes. At present, according to IRS data, the top income quintile (20%) in America earns on average almost 8 times as much as our poorest quintile. In Japan the ratio is 5 to 1, and their economy hasn't suffered. I resist thinking in terms of wealth redistribution, but it's an alternative worth considering.

· The number of people giving and serving and the number of hours expended both need to increase. The nonprofit sector will need to reallocate priorities and rechannel resources. But it must remain innovative and experimental, developing new and better programs. It should not simply fill in the holes missed by the big-government paving machine.

· Our best economists, environmentalists, philanthropists, and government leaders should join experts from all over the world to prioritize issues and pledge resources. The economically advanced nations should play a significant financial role in renewing the social and economic structures of disadvantaged nations. These nations cannot, with present resources, overcome their problems. Advanced nations must be prepared to provide emergency aid and resources to move disadvantaged nations to a state of self-sufficiency.

A New World Leadership

The sole meaning of life is to serve humanity.
Leo Tolstoy

What kinds of leaders can help the world move forward through all its manifold social and environmental problems? I believe we need a shift in the paradigms of leadership. Instead of pursuing power and gain for nations and for themselves, leaders need to seek solutions to the great crises of the world.

The world has too little enlightened leadership. Too many leaders are nationalistic in their approach to global problems. This is lamentable, but I don't think that too much blame need be attached to it. After all, politics and statesmanship exist to protect, expand, and promote the economic and political aims of individual countries. Leaders to a large extent merely reflect the motives of the populace. I can't recall any warlike, aggressive nation ever electing a pacifist leader. The basic motives that guide an advanced nation are economic and personal gain. In less advanced countries, benevolence and cooperation are often displaced by naked aggression and the desire for power.

Leadership frequently amounts to the unbridled practice of power for personal gain. Desire for power and raw ambition are more often the prerequisites to leadership than compassion and humility. The noted religious leader Dr. John Haggai in his book *Lead On* says, "Love as a characteristic of leadership seems to be out of place, yet there cannot be true leadership without love. The love of which I speak . . . is the outgoing of the totality of one's being to another in beneficence and help." The mind of the politician is complex, and leadership is often a reward for long-time service in the ranks of a political party. Politics rarely rewards humanitarian impulses.

Of course, not all world and national leaders are venal. Their dilemma is that they have a constituency to serve; their task is to satisfy the needs of those who put them in power. They are often forced to make decisions that penalize, disenfranchise, or limit support for their nation's most impoverished and troubled people. Sometimes they are pressured to make decisions that go *against* common respect for human rights and compassionate concern. Private interests and a desire for power are usually close to the throne. Anyone who has been a student of leadership knows that leaders are subject to all sorts of frailties.

I find it difficult to believe that a leader who commits his nation to a war of aggression can also have a deep compassion for his nation's disadvantaged. It's hard to understand how war can be beneficial to any populace or environment. A war machine drains funds that could be employed to resolve social ills. Yet supremacy and dominance are the goals of many nations, and many of the world's leaders achieved their positions by aligning themselves with the powerful, the ambitious, and the driven. Such leaders are not the most sensitive, compassionate clan on the face of the earth.

Today more than ever we need leaders who can plan and manage the process of healing our wounded planet. Establishing sensible, reasonable goals and prioritizing the problems to be faced call for the talents of the most skilled and humane individuals—not those wedded to seats of power or rigid ideologies. The new leadership will need great sensitivity and the ability to gain cooperation from the uncaring and unwilling. This leadership must somehow balance the need for economic progress and national security amid political and social turbulence. The task of reconstruction will be most demanding.

If this mission is to be successful, it cannot be left in the hands of those who favor power and self-gain. We need to empower experts in the arts of sacrifice, mediation, compassion, perseverance, persuasiveness, and planning. In trying to restructure many of the world's most fragile and troubled economies, these new leaders will have to do battle with the entrenched and protective interests of the world. They will be downsizing or dismantling many war machines. And most critical of all, they will be asking nations to set aside sovereign rule and cooperate with policies that may run counter to their immediate interests.

Such leaders will need diplomacy, tact, perseverance, and deftness. Their tasks will require the perspective and vision of world planners, not the insular restrictive myopia of chauvinistic politicians or governmental bureaucrats. But these leaders will also need to harness governmental efforts to accomplish the tasks of reconstruction.

How can any body of humane, intelligent, and qualified leaders adequately evaluate the world's tragedies and miseries, assign priorities, and prescribe remedies? Nations have found few remedies to social ills and even fewer to environmental problems. History is filled with conflict, strife, and war but very few humane cooperative ventures. The United Nations and its predecessor, the League of Nations, were to be forums to facilitate peace, but their track records have been less than inspiring. Somehow nations must be convinced that global cooperation and planning are the only sane courses of action.

Time is running out. There must be an unequivocal commitment by each nation to devote much of its resources and manpower to the reconstruction of global

imbalances and the correction of internal ills. So far fragmented programs, world conflict, and war have defeated
efforts to remedy our many troubles. Some programs, like
the Marshall Plan at the end of World War II, have worked
and worked well. As we did then, so today we have the
resources to end our social and environmental troubles.
But first we must overcome economic and political interests, the quick fix mentality, and crippling nationalism
and aggression. Early progress will likely spring from educational efforts. World leaders and the public at large
must be made fully aware of the disastrous state of the
world and the economic, political, and social excesses that
have led us to this global crisis.

Who can we turn to for such an assignment? The
answer is: everyone. All nations must inform their citizens
of the nature and extent of our problems. Government
leaders must extract concessions from their citizens to
permit cooperation on a world basis. They also need to
commit some of their resources to global reconstruction.
If only a few nations agree to such a course of action, the
renewal effort won't work. The problems are too exten-
sive. Many nations will need to commit to two broad
agendas:

1. To pledge some of their resources and manpower to
   assist other nations and help reverse world environmental imbalances.
2. To pledge a significant proportion of national resources and manpower to correct and eliminate internal social and environmental ills. For some of the
   poorest nations, this will require aid and technical
   assistance from abroad.

Willingness to cooperate and a firm commitment by
each government to follow the reconstruction plan will be
essential building blocks in any renewal effort.

New Leaders

To begin this gigantic effort, I propose a global task force of philanthropists, economists, business leaders, governmental experts, statesmen, environmentalists, scientists, medical experts, sociologists. This umbrella task force should assess the current and future impact of each social and environmental problem at both the national and international levels. It will assign priorities and design relief and renewal programs in cooperation with national governments.

Implementation of the plans will have to be borne by the individual countries with their own resources or with international aid. The task force should also evaluate each nation's resources and abilities to contribute to other, less fortunate nations. Implicit in this global approach is a relinquishing of some national control, a commitment of resources, and a willingness to plan and execute in an ecumenical spirit.

There is risk and uncertainty in any plan this size, of course, and the success of this global program will depend upon the reactions and commitments of the superpower nations and the wisdom of their leaders. Success will involve a significant redistribution of the world's wealth and resources and quite a bit of sacrifice. But disease, famine, poverty, and faltering ecosystems will not diminish on their own. Misery will expand and grow unless we band together in one universal effort.

In America, we must evaluate our potential leaders in terms of their sensitivity to the needs of the disadvantaged. In the past we have not always selected the most humane leaders. We need to be clear about the role we want our elected representatives to play. They control taxation and the national budget.

As individuals, we collectively have the power to shift

priorities and resources. We can, if we choose, contain those who trash the environment or allocate huge sums to the military. We can use our energies to advocate, lobby, vote, inform, rally, educate, and support the causes we believe in.

Who will finally lead us into global recovery? My answer is . . . *you*, a person who has discovered the life-enhancing benefits of daily practice of the Golden Rule. *You*, a person who gives to live and in so doing changes the lives of others as you change your own.

T·W·E·L·V·E

TREADING
THE GIVING PATH

There is nothing new about the Giving Path. Literally millions of people through the ages have understood intuitively that the way to their own health, happiness, and peace of mind lay in helping others. Giving and sharing have always been the way wise men and women have built the world, for others and for themselves.

What is new is our understanding of how philanthropy affects our bodies and minds. The extraordinary findings of the last two decades of research enable us to say with assurance what we always suspected was true: to give is to live.

When we give our time, our money, our talent, our concern, and our compassion for others to a cause, we receive more than we give. Our hearts, our immune systems, and our general health all improve. Our minds are clearer and more focussed, we have a better and more positive picture of ourselves, and we are better able to sort out and meet the competing demands of our lives. We feel better about ourselves, we know we are loved and we can love all the more in return. We change for the better when we help other people, and at the same time we change their lives and the world.

There are ways to become involved in giving and sharing that help us get the greatest return—physically, mentally, and emotionally—from our investment of time and treasure. The first thing we need to remember is that *our lives are important*, what we value is important, and therefore we can choose causes to make the best use of what we have to offer. Our time is important, and so there are ways to incorporate sharing into our daily routine. We *can* do what we set out to do if we are honest about what we want and feel, and if we plan to make the best use of what we have.

The Giving Path is a path to family renewal. We can begin by sharing what we have, and then enlist our wives or husbands, children, even parents and brothers and sisters in our causes. Children learn to lead wholesome and generous lives by being encouraged to take the Giving Path early in life. Young people are brought to a greater respect for others and themselves by helping and sharing. We learn how we can make the greatest possible use of what God has given us in this life so that our values can continue to shape the world after we are gone.

When we walk the Giving Path, we release tremendous power in our own lives. The power we may have looked for—by heaping up wealth or manipulating others—we can find when we help others. Our lives begin to blossom when we follow the spiritual principle of "doing unto others as we would have them do unto us." And we experience a powerful integration of the different forces in our lives as we channel much of our drives for power and control into the work of sharing and giving.

In praising, acknowledging, and recognizing others we discover that we unleash their energies for good and create powerful human networks that can accomplish tremendous things. A generous response to others enables us to see that they are indeed "points of light" giving us, our children, and our friends models of what we might do ourselves. Sharing our troubles with others in like circumstances helps us learn from one another and points a way out of the despair that our addictions and afflictions can lead us into.

When we begin to help others, our hearts will grow and our minds will inevitably awaken to the tremendous needs of people around the world and to the degradation of our planet's environment. The Giving Path helps us become aware of terrible realities yet at the same time empowers us to improve our society and the world. The growing problems in America and abroad compel each of us to try to find solutions. And when situations call for changes in political and economic structures, as they surely will, we will find that the generosity of heart we learned on the Giving Path will give us the strength and courage to face the changes with equanimity and grace.

Giving to live is in fact the only way to live fully. When each of us shares what has been given to us, we gain a new life. If each of us hangs onto what we have, it will never seem enough. Even the richest people in the world think they have to have more if they do not have the habit of sharing what they have. They are letting what they have determine who they are.

The loving energy of a person like St. Francis of Assisi or Mother Teresa of Calcutta can transform the world, even if he or she doesn't possess a dime. What they do have is the indomitable human spirit given by their Creator, and so they are endowed with almost limitless potential. You possess that same spirit. When you walk the Giving Path, when you give to live, your spirit will expand, your powers will grow, and you will be able to bring about great things.

The material gifts we are given never seem enough until we have shared them with others. When we give to a good cause, we are linked with others—in the solidarity of giving but also in the solidarity of human need, because every human being needs something. When we are in solidarity with each other, we learn what our real needs are. Our lives become more focussed, and we value the good things we have earned or been given all the more because we see what they have been able to accomplish. Our lives are simplified and our spirits strengthened when we give. Sharing puts us back in touch with each other.

Most of all, walking the Giving Path connects us to the great Giver himself. We know that it is God's nature to give and give without measure or complaint, even when His gift and His love are ignored or abused. His overflowing love is what makes the world and our own lives possible. So when we feed a hungry man, when we help a child learn to read, when we help fund a clinic, when we give clothing for the poor, we are connecting ourselves to the love of God. We are increasing and multiplying the giving energy of the divine in the world. We are helping bring about the Kingdom of Heaven on earth.

Giving is living. Without the gift of life from our parents, we would not exist. Without their nurture when we were infants, without help from society as we went to school and grew in stature and knowledge, without the help of others (often strangers to us) as our careers and lives unfold, we would have no life. Everything we are and everything we have is a gift. What little we have earned— and it can never be enough to pay back the entire gift given us—we are called to invest in each other.

Giving is living because in giving our lives are made better in every conceivable way. When we give to others, when we share our time, talent, and treasure, we do not end up with less in our accounts, but more.

So I call on you to begin a life of giving. Walk the Giving Path. Share what you have with others. Let your light shine. Give as you have been given to, and more will be given to you, in greater measure, pressed down, and overflowing. Join the Giver and all his human helpers through the ages. Your life will never be the same.

BIBLIOGRAPHY

Allen, Derek. *A Comparative Study of the Tax Treatment of Donors to Charity in Various Countries.* Tonbridge, Kent, England: Charities Aid Foundation, 1987.

"Altruism's Own Rewards." *Foundation News.* Washington DC, May-June 1988, 29ff.

"A Time to Seek." *Newsweek,* December 17, 1990.

Autry, James A. *Love and Profit.* New York: William Morrow & Co., 1991.

"A Windfall Nears in Inheritances from the Richest Generation." *The New York Times,* July 22, 1990, p. 4.

Bellah, Robert. *Habits of the Heart.* Berkeley: University of California Press, 1985.

Benson, Herbert. *The Mind/Body Effect.* New York: Simon & Schuster, 1979.

_____. *The Relaxation Response.* Boston: G. K. Hall, 1976.

Blanchard, Kenneth and Johnson, Spencer. *The One-Minute Manager.* New York: William Morrow, 1982.

"Breaking a Spring Tradition," *USA Today,* March 15, 1991, p. D-1.

Bremner, Robert H. *American Philanthropy.* Chicago: University of Chicago Press, 1988.

Burns, David D. *Feeling Good: The New Mood Therapy.* New York: William Morrow, 1980.

Buscaglia, Leo D. *Loving Each Other.* New York: Holt, Rinehart and Winston, 1984.

Carlson, Martin. *Why People Give.* New York: Council Press, 1985.

Castro, Janice, "The Simple Life." *Time,* (April 8, 1991), pp. 58-63.

Chambre, Susan Maizel. *Good Deeds in Old Age.* Lexington, MA: Lexington Books, 1987.

"Charitable Giving and Philanthropy Soared from 1987 to 1989." *The Chronicle of Philanthropy.* Washington, DC, October 16, 1990.

Charitable Giving: What Contributors Want to Know. New York: National Charities Information Bureau, 1988.

Cohen, Lilly and Young, Dennis, editors. *Careers for Dreamers and Doers: A Guide to Management Careers in the Non-Profit Sector.* New York: Foundation Center, 1989.

Cornuelle, Richard. *Healing America.* New York: G. P. Putnam, 1983.

_____. *Reclaiming the American Dream.* New York: Random House, 1965.

Cousins, Norman. *Anatomy of an Illness.* Boston: G. K. Hall, 1979.

_____. *Head First: The Biology of Hope.* New York: Dutton, 1989.

Csikszentmihalyi, Mihaly. *Flow: The Psychology of Optimal Experience.* New York: Harper and Row, 1990.

Daring Goals for a Caring Society: A Blueprint for Substantial Growth in Giving and Volunteering in America. Washington DC: Independent Sector, 1986.

Dass, Ram and Gorman, Paul. *How Can I Help? Stories and Reflections on Service.* New York: Alfred A. Knopf, 1985.

De Tocqueville, Alexis. *Democracy in America.* New York: Viking, 1956.

Douglas, James. *Why Charity? The Case for the Third Sector.* Beverly Hills CA: Sage Publications, 1983.

Drotning, Philip. *Putting the Fun in Fund Raising.* New York: Contemporary Books, 1979.

Dunn, Thomas. *How to Shake the New Money Tree.* New York: Viking Penguin, Inc., 1988.

Erikson, Eric H. *Childhood and Society.* New York: W. W. Norton, 1950.

_____. *Identity and Life Cycle.* New York: W. W. Norton, 1980.

Emrika, Padus. *The Complete Guide to Your Emotions and Your Health.* Emmaus PA: Rodale Press, 1986.

Frantzreb, Arthur C. "Philanthropy is Both Giving and Receiving." *Fund Raising Management,* January 1984.

Frankl, Victor. *Man's Search for Meaning.* New York: Washington Square, 1963.

Gallup Organization. *Religion in America.* Report 259. Princeton, NJ: Gallup Organization, April 1987.

Gallup Survey. *Non-Profit Times.* November 1988, 2(8), p. 1.

Gaylin, William. *Caring.* New York: Alfred Knopf, 1983.

"Giving and Volunteering in the United States." Washington DC: Independent Sector, 1988.

Giving USA, The Annual Report on Philanthropy for the Year 1989. New York: AAFRC Trust for Philanthropy, 1990.

Gordon, Sol and Brecher, Harold. *Life is Uncertain, Eat Dessert First!* New York: Delacorte Press, 1990.

Haggai, John. *Lead On.* Waco TX: Word Books, 1986.

Handlin, Oscar and Handlin, Mary. *The Wealth of the American People: A History of American Affluence.* New York: McGraw-Hill, 1975.

The Health Benefits of Helping. Washington DC: Spring Research Forum, Independent Sector, 1989.

Hodgkinson, Virginia. *Dimensions of the Independent Sector: A Statistical Profile.* Washington: Independent Sector, 1984, 1986.

_____. *Dimensions of the Independent Sector: A Statistical Profile.* New York: Foundation Center, 1990.

Hodgkinson, Virginia and Wuthnow, Robert. *Faith and Philanthropy in America.* San Francisco: Jossey-Bass, 1990.

Jaffe, Dennis. *From Burnout to Balance.* New York: McGraw-Hill, 1984.

_____. *Healing From Within.* New York: Alfred Knopf, 1980.

James, Estelle. *The Non-Profit Sector in International Perspective.* New Haven CT: Institution for Social and Policy Studies, 1980.

Jampolsky, Gerald. *Out of Darkness into the Light: A Journey of Inner Healing.* New York: Bantam Books, 1989.

Joseph, James. *The Charitable Impulse.* Washington, D.C.: Council on Foundations, 1989.

"Learning to Give." *US Air Magazine,* December 1990, 42ff.

Lewin, David. "Community Involvement, Employee Morale and Business Performance: A Study of U.S. Companies," New York: Working Papers, 1991.

Luks, Allan. "Helper's High." *Psychology Today,* October 1988, 38ff.

Lynch, James. *The Broken Heart: The Medical Consequences of Loneliness.* New York: Basic, 1979.

Magat, Richard. *Old Wine or Potent Brew.* Unpublished, 1989.

———, editor. *Philanthropic Giving: Studies in Varieties and Goals.* Yale Studies on Nonprofit Organizations. New York: Oxford University Press, 1989.

Marts, Arnaud. *The Generosity of Americans.* Englewood Cliffs NJ: Prentice-Hall, Inc., 1966.

———. *Philanthropy's Role in Civilization.* New York: Harper & Row, 1953.

Maslow, Abraham. *Religious Values and Peak Experiences.* New York: Viking, 1970.

May, Rollo. *Man's Search for Himself.* New York: W. W. Norton & Co., 1953.

Measurable Growth in Giving and Volunteering. Washington DC: Independent Sector, 1985.

Millar, Bruce. "Baby Boomers Give Generously to Their Charities, Survey Finds, But Their Willingness to do Volunteer Work is Questioned," *The Chronicle of Philanthropy,* July 24, 1990.

Montague, Peter and Montague, Katherine. *No World Without End.* New York: G. P. Putnam's Sons, 1976.

Nichols, Judith. *Changing Demographics: Fund Raising in the 1990's.* Chicago: Pluribus Press, 1990.

O'Connell, Brian. *America's Voluntary Spirit.* New York: Foundation Center, 1983.

_____. *Philanthropy in Action*. New York: Foundation Center, 1987.

_____. *Volunteers in Action*. New York: Foundation Center, 1990.

Odendahl, Teresa. *Charity Begins at Home: Generosity and Self Interest Among the Philanthropic Elite*. New York: Basic Books, 1990.

O'Neill, Michael. *The Third America: The Emergence of the Nonprofit Sector in the United States*. San Francisco: Jossey-Bass, 1989.

Ornish, Dean. *A Program for Reversing Heart Disease*. New York: Random House, 1990.

_____. "The Healing Power of Love," *Prevention Magazine*, February 1991, pp. 60f.

Ornstein, Robert and Sobel, David. *The Healing Brain*. New York: Simon and Schuster, 1987.

_____. *Healthy Pleasures*. Reading MA: Addison-Wesley Publishing, 1989.

Panas, Jerold. *Born To Raise: What Makes a Great Fundraiser, What Makes a Fundraiser Great*. Chicago: Pluribus Press, 1988.

_____. *Megagifts*. Chicago: Pluribus Press, 1984.

_____. *Official Fundraising Almanac*. Chicago: Pluribus Press, 1989.

Pare, Terrence. "Passing on the Family Business," *Fortune*, May 1990, p. 81f.

Payton, Robert. *Philanthropy: Voluntary Action for the Public Good*. New York: Macmillan, 1988.

Peale, Norman Vincent. *How to Make Positive Imaging Work for You*. Old Tappan NJ: Fleming Revell Co., 1982.

_____. *Power of the Plus Factor*. Old Tappan NJ: Fleming Revell Co., 1987.

Peck, M. Scott. *The Different Drum*. New York: Simon & Schuster, 1980.

_____. *The Road Less Traveled*. New York: Simon & Schuster, 1987.

"Private Students Volunteer: The Privileged Aid the Poor." *The New York Times* (April 4, 1991), p. A-16.

"Pro-Social Behavior." *Psychology Today*, October 1988, p. 34ff.

Rockefeller, John D. 3rd. *The Second American Revolution.* New York: Harper & Row, 1973.

Rogers, Carl. *On Becoming A Person.* Boston: Houghton-Mifflin Company, 1961.

Sacks, Oliver. *Awakenings.* New York: Harper Collins Publishers, 1973.

Schuller, Robert. *The Be-Happy Attitudes.* Waco TX: Word Books, 1985.

Selye, Hans. *The Stress of Life.* New York: McGraw-Hill, 1976.

_____. *Stress Without Distress.* Philadelphia: Lippincott, 1974.

"Seven Steps to Happiness." *Psychology Today*, July/August 1989, 37ff.

Sheehy, Gail. *Passages: Predictable Crises of Adult Life.* New York: E. P. Dutton, 1976.

Siegel, Bernie S. *Love, Medicine and Miracles.* New York: Harper & Row, 1986.

Simon, Sidney B. *Getting Unstuck.* New York: Warner Books, 1988.

_____. *Values Clarification.* New York: Hart Publishing, 1972.

Stokes, Bruce. *Helping Ourselves: Local Solutions to Global Problems.* New York: W. W. Norton & Co., 1981.

"The ABC's of Philanthropy: First Lesson Is Well Learned," *The New York Times*, March 15, 1991, p. A-16.

"The *New York Times* Neediest Cases," *The New York Times*, December 17, 1990.

Vaillant, George. *Adaptation to Life.* Boston: Little, Brown, 1977.

Van Til, John et al. *Critical Issues in American Philanthropy.* New York: AAFRC Trust for Philanthropy, 1990.

_____. *Mapping the Third Sector: Voluntarism in a Changing Social Economy.* New York: Foundation Center, 1988.